WORK
WOULD BE
GREAT

IF IT WEREN'T FOR THE PEOPLE

D0029474

WORK WOULD BE GREAT

IF IT WEREN'T FOR THE PEOPLE

Making Office Politics Work for You

by Ronna Lichtenberg
with Gene Stone

HYPERION

NEW YORK

Library of Congress Cataloging-in-Publication Data

Lichtenberg, Ronna

    Work would be great if it weren't for the people: making office politics work
for you / by Ronna Lichtenberg with Gene Stone.
        p.   cm.
    ISBN 0-7868-8407-X
    1. Office politics,   I. Stone, Gene   II. Title.
HF5386.5.L53   1998
650.1'3—dc21

                                        97-46836
                                          CIP

Designed by Robert Bull Design

First Paperback Edition

10 9 8 7 6 5 4 3 2 1

For Jimmy

TABLE OF CONTENTS

OFFICE POLITICS: AN INTRODUCTION

"Work would be great if it weren't for the people."
—EVERYBODY

Do you believe that . . .

- sexual attraction in the office is a non-issue?

- cronyism doesn't exist?

- bonuses, raises, and perks are determined solely by performance?

- other people always play fair?

- logic prevails in disputes over organizational boundaries?

- whether or not you're offered a good job is determined by a rational assessment of whether or not you deserve it?

- you can safely ignore what your co-workers say about you?

- you can do your job well without anyone else's cooperation?

- it doesn't matter if your colleague's spouse plays a regular tennis game with the boss's spouse?

Of course you don't.
Why?
Because you know that, although it doesn't seem fair, talent

alone isn't enough. Nor is hard work. Or reliability, or an overflowing Rolodex, or an Ivy League pedigree, for that matter.

No matter what you do, which product you make, or how many services you render, without other people you're not doing business. Without other people there *is* no business.

Every time something goes right—an order is placed, an account is won, a project is completed—it's because people got the job done.

Likewise, when something goes wrong—an order is misplaced, an account is lost, a project collapses, it's because somewhere along the line people dropped the ball.

So if business is about people, and you're in business, then people is what you're about, too, no matter what you make or sell or service. Unless you've somehow found a way to work in a vacuum, your fortunes at work are inexorably linked with the fortunes of all those around you. That unhappy man at the end of the corridor who signs off on expense accounts, that elderly secretary who watches over your boss like a mother hen, that pleasant security guard who opens the building for you late at night: All these people affect what you do. Always. All the time. And forever.

This means, like it or not, that you're already playing office politics.

If you scoff at this, if you laugh and say that you're not into playing games, that you're above such silliness, then you're already losing at politics. Because no one can survive at any organization on skill alone.

Given that, here's the bottom line: **It's okay to be good at politics.** All politics really boils down to is the play of human interactions at work that can make your job either easier or more difficult. That's it. So why not be as good as possible? Never mind that the word *politics* has developed a terrible connotation. Excuse the fact that it sounds demeaning. It's okay to become a good office politician.

And anyone can learn, once you admit that it's a necessary component of the job.

Excelling at office politics doesn't necessarily involve injuries or pain. **Only a small minority of people are out to succeed at all cost, and this book isn't for them.** This book is for everyone else who works for a living and who wants to further his or her success by understanding more about the human element of the workplace.

If office politics, in practice, can be so good, why does nearly everyone find the idea so objectionable?

For instance: Not long ago I was talking to Mark, a quiet, ambitious young employee of mine who had found himself in the middle of a minor crisis. Believing that a co-worker was jeopardizing a project on which they were collaborating, Mark dashed off a self-exonerating memo to the Big Boss explaining how the other guy was screwing up. Even though Mark was technically correct, airing the problem made everyone look bad. The boss was angry, the co-worker was resentful, and Mark realized he'd stepped into a political morass.

When I asked him why someone so smart had been inspired to do something so dumb, Mark shrugged and answered, "Hey, you know me. I tell it as I see it. I'm no good at politics." He announced this proudly, which is how most people express their disregard for office politics. In Mark's mind his inability to conceal his impatience with a rival meant that he was somehow morally superior.

Mark was wrong. The impulse to draft an angry memo is understandable. But to send it without thinking—that's a foolish move. Checking his anger wouldn't have meant a moral compromise, and it would have been more practical, as it would have made it easier for Mark and his colleague to fix the underlying problem.

That's the essence of good politics: Negotiating individual agendas so the work can get done.

You'd never know that, though, from the ways office politics is portrayed in contemporary culture. The popular image of an office politician is a slimeball, a plotter and schemer who doesn't care at all about real work, someone who makes trouble for others while thinking only of himself or herself.

Go to the movies. In *Jerry Maguire*, you know who the good guy is when he posts a mission statement for his office with the same rectitude as Martin Luther posting his Ninety-five Theses. The bad guys? The ones who prophesy the dire political consequences of Maguire's noble effort. In *Working Girl*, Sigourney Weaver's character is so unrepentantly bad that the audience cheers when her assistant steals her lingerie, her fiancé, and her job, all because the younger woman was the victim of bad politics, thus justifying her revenge. This bias isn't limited to the movies: in books and on television, bad people are always playing bad politics. They deserve bad endings.

Popular culture has in effect managed to separate work from politics. First there's work: this pure, holy thing that we all like to think we've mastered. Then there's politics, which keeps us from doing what we define as work. Politics is the bogeyman. It's politics that keeps the boss from approving your brilliant piece of copy. It's politics that keeps your salary low, politics that gets your rivals promoted.

Sometimes, in fact, the problem really *is* them. At other times it's us. At still other times it lies in the fact that we're all not talking to each other, or recognizing difficulties early on, or understanding how human emotions can clog up an office the way hair stops up a drain.

If you knew more about office politics, you could make the distinction and you could perform your job more effectively and efficiently—and maintain your sanity as well.

I happen to be pretty good when it comes to politics. I should be—I've worked at it since my first job at the age of twelve in a local bar (it was actually my father's place); all throughout my career in Washington, D.C.; and then as I climbed the ropes up to senior vice president for External Affairs at Prudential Securities in New York. And even I smart when people praise me for my political prowess; it sounds like a backhanded compliment implying my actual work is somehow deficient.

But when I say I'm good at politics, what I mean is that I try to understand the agendas of people around me (including my own), and attempt to coordinate our efforts to create the best possible result. **Being a good office politician means that you know how to turn individual agendas into common goals.** You become a facilitator. You empower other people to achieve great things.

Not that office politics can't be abused. There are always going to be some people who only play politics for their own gain. If that's you, you'd better do your dirty work fast and be prepared to move on, because the organization will smell what you are—a predator—and will rally against you for its own protection.

THE EVIL TWIN

As an expert on office politics, I get many calls and letters asking for advice. This one came from Minneapolis:

Dear Ronna,

I hate writing letters. I hate receiving them. But what the hell. I run the news department of a television station. It's tough and it's low budget but what makes it work are the people. There's Murray, who's a damn good writer, and we've got a dim bulb named Ted reading the news, but he gets good ratings. And then there's Mary, who's great. Period. I gave her her start.

We also have this dame Sue Ann, and that's the issue. Sue Ann's a bitch. So what if I slept with her once? It was an accident. Anyway, she's our Happy Homemaker, and every day after lunch—at 2:50, to be exact—she's happy because she and the station's chief financial officer are having sex. On her set just before the show starts, at three o'clock.

Worse, the man controls the purse strings, and so he told me I've got to give Sue Ann all the bonus money this year, which means there's nothing for anyone else. I don't care about the money myself, but Mary needs it for her sick parents, Murray's saving to put his kids through college, and Ted's girlfriend Georgette was hoping this would give Ted the means to marry her. Sue Ann's using her money to enlarge her breasts.

What the hell do I do?

Yours,

Lou

Here's my reply:

Dear Lou,

It sounds as though your happy Sue Ann's gone a little too far. You have two choices. One is to go to the station manager and demand she be fired, which will get you into a battle with the CFO. Only you know if you're powerful enough to survive that.

The second option is to listen to your Evil Twin and take matters into your own hands. If you want to succeed at business, there are times when you have to accept your Evil Twin's advice.

Here's what my Evil Twin suggests to yours. Go down to Sue Ann's set and turn her display clocks back ten minutes. Then bribe one of the camera men to film whatever he sees at three o'clock. They probably hate her anyway. Tell him to make sure he's operating by his watch, not Sue Ann's clock. Then when the CFO shows up, Sue Ann will get into position and all of Minneapolis will get to watch. The CFO will soon be gone, and then Mary's parents can get well, Murray's kids can go to college, and Ted and Georgette can get married.

Good luck,

Ronna

Like Lou, everyone hates aspects of his or her job. Who hasn't felt victimized, underappreciated, or bullied by a boss, co-worker, or enemy during his or her career? It feels as if there's nothing you can do about it. It feels as if it's always been like this. And on really bad days, it feels as if it always will be.

In a way, this isn't a new experience. Think back to the first time you encountered this kind of bullying. You were being tormented by some creep in grade school. It started with taunts, but it escalated. In a fair world, you could have hit him back. But the guy was twice your size. In a fair world, you could have appealed to the teacher. But then you'd have run the risk of being labeled a tattletale, and besides, your tormentor only would have gotten even angrier. Your only hope was to make sure that the kid ended up in detention every day for as long as possible. You'd have done anything to arrange it. So you listened to the side of you that knew how to cause that bully some real grief— no matter what it took. After all, you wanted to keep your teeth.

Now it's thirty years later, and someone's bullying you at the office. He's sleeping with your boss, or stealing your ideas, or lying about what you did or didn't say. It's still not a fair world. You have no court of appeals, no one to protect your interests. So what do you do? You listen to that same Evil Twin who managed to get that bully stuck in detention all year.

The concept of the Evil Twin first occurred to me when I realized that every time something bad happened to me at work, I'd hear two internal voices: one mature, rational, and thoughtful; the other focused exclusively on revenge. One said, "Let's work this out quietly and sensibly." The other said, "I'm mad as hell and I'm going to do something about it." That second voice was my Evil Twin, screaming for a chance to get out and get even.

Everyone has an Evil Twin. Every one of us. And all day that Evil Twin is talking to us. The Evil Twin never stops thinking up ways to help. There you are, sitting calmly at your desk, when you come across a memo with some information your enemy desperately needs. No one knows you have it. What do you do? "Burn it," whispers your Evil Twin.

Or perhaps you use the information for your own benefit. Or perhaps you engage in other favorite Evil Twin activities, such as passing along news that should be kept quiet. "Did I tell you that Will just went back to school?" your Evil Twin confides in the person most likely to tell the boss. "I bet he really will get his degree this time."

And what about distorting information? Or not communicating the truth, or ganging up on people, or undermining authority? The Evil Twin is remarkably creative.

Most of the time you mustn't accept your Evil Twin's advice. Instead, take the high road: Dig deeper into the issue, make an effort to understand everyone's concerns, work to discover why things went awry, and attempt to find a solution that works for everyone.

But now and then you're provoked beyond reason and fairness, and you need to fight back. That's when it's time to listen to the Evil Twin carefully—and, perhaps, even act on its advice. I've certainly done it: Several years ago Hank, a co-worker and peer, informed me that our boss's boss wanted to make him the head of a new department. Hank didn't know I despised him. It wasn't just me—everyone did. And we had good reasons: Hank was the kind of guy who as a kid practiced his management style by tying tin cans to animals' tails.

So I thought about what he'd said, and soon enough my Evil Twin appeared. "Don't let this happen—it'll ruin the department and a lot of careers—stop him."

I couldn't act directly to prevent his promotion, but I could help Hank follow his own narcissistic instincts: I recommended he share his good news with our boss *before* it became official. Our boss didn't like Hank, either, and I knew being left out of the loop would anger him.

Hank, too flushed with success to foresee a problem, went ahead and told the boss, who, as predicted, erupted. Hank's promotion was derailed, and his career didn't quite get back onto the fast track.

In this case, I listened to my Evil Twin for what I believed was a good reason, and I'm not sorry I did.

That's the only justification for following your Evil Twin's advice: **If you believe that upon later reflection you'll still be content with your actions.** You don't let your Evil Twin prevail just because you're feeling mean-spirited. When you decide to act on your Evil Twin's suggestions, thoroughly think through what you're doing and why you're doing it.

Aren't I justifying being both judge and executioner? Yes. As do the hundreds of others I've talked to about politics and their occasional use of their own Evil Twins. In certain situations, there's simply no alternative.

But you must be cautious when enlisting your Evil Twin's help. If your Twin is out of control, the result will be unmitigated chaos, which is why you must always obey the conditions of the Evil Twin Code of Honor:

- **Strict discipline is required.** The Evil Twin is a weapon that can be employed only upon careful reflection. Acting rashly on your Evil Twin's guidance almost always leads to tragedy.

- **Use your Evil Twin only in self-defense.** Your job at the office is to get the work done as best you know how. Your job is to make things happen. Use your Evil Twin exclusively in those moments when someone is blocking your own momentum. Think of it as a kind of mental judo that helps you turn other people's bad energy back against them.

- **Don't lie about facts.** The moment you start lying, you and your Evil Twin both lose. If your lies are uncovered—and most lies are—no one will ever believe you again.
- **Exercise discretion.** If you feel you must take action, pick your time and place wisely. Public confrontations never end well; they disturb the office's equilibrium and they make everyone look bad—especially you.
- **Don't burn civilians.** Example: Your enemy, Fred, takes a small apartment in the city, supposedly to cut down on his commute. Still, Fred's out of work every evening at 7 P.M. But when you see Fred's wife, she tells you how worried she is about Fred, what with him working every night until midnight. Your Evil Twin wants to play dumb: "Fred? But he leaves every day by seven—with his assistant." Don't do it. There's nothing to be gained by bombing civilian targets—except wrath.
- **Screen your Evil Twin carefully.** The Evil Twin loves to talk, and there's no harm in listening—but you act on its advice only when left with no other choice. You should be able to remember every time you've used your Evil Twin's counsel. If you can't, then you're overdoing it.

Whether or not you choose to heed it, your Evil Twin has a powerful voice—and a strong opinion on—virtually every subject. You'll find this predilection for unsolicited advice reflected throughout this book; like it or not, the Evil Twin has something to say about practically every move you make in the workplace. The key: Never act on these suggestions if it means violating the Code of Honor.

Given the reputation of office politics today, it's not a good idea to be publically acknowledged as an accomplished politician. Someday, when the subject is less taboo, perhaps they'll start giving awards for this skill at company dinners. In the meantime, if your co-workers notice that you're acting in what they consider to be a political manner, they may become frightened and/or feel manipulated.

My personal ethic holds that if you discuss your plans openly, it's not manipulative. I'll always say, "I want to get this done, and here's what I want to do. Step one, step two, step three, and so on." I make sure that everyone involved knows. So by my rules, this isn't manipulation. **It's not magic if you know how the trick works.**

But don't expect praise for mastering this sport. If you're doing it right, people won't consider you a politician, but rather an effective worker. The bottom line is to be so good at politics that people notice nothing more than the fact that things get done a little more easily when you're involved and no one seems to get hurt in the process. That's the praise you can expect to receive: You're not only good at your job, you're good at making other people good at their jobs, too. As a result, your whole office runs more smoothly.

Some people are born politicians, smooth operators from the moment they learn to smile. Career diplomats, they sail through work (and life) seemingly effortlessly. But if you're like most people, you have your good days and your bad. You can deal with some co-workers but have written off others. In short, there's room for improvement, but you don't know where, or how, to begin.

If you're curious about your innate political capabilities, try the following test, which features three work-related situations and a range of political responses. Total up your score and see where you fall in the gamut.

1. For many years you were employed at a major Hollywood talent agency, working for Mr. Smith, the most important player in the business. Then you went off on your own. But recently Mr.

Smith left the agency himself to take a job as the number-two person at Major Studios and hired you. You quickly became known as Smith's person, although your relationship wasn't actually that close. Still, it made you feel good—until rumors started circulating that Smith was in trouble.

One day you're sitting at your desk when an enemy—a great ally of Smith's boss, the Chairman—calls you with the news: The Chairman has booted Smith out of Major Studios.

What do you do?

A. Pretend that someone's just come into your office and quickly hang up.

B. Proclaim that the Chairman has always been your favorite executive—thank God he's still on top.

C. Moan and confess that you feel Smith was just too damn good for Major Studios and that this is a real tragedy.

D. Ask where Smith is going.

Answers:

If you said B, you'll look like an idiot. No one's going to believe your sudden shift in loyalty. Score yourself -2 points.

If you said C, you may think you're coming across as loyal, but in fact you're being disloyal to the company structure, and your enemy will pass along this fact to the powers that be. Anyway, you have no real friends at work (see You've Got to Have Friends . . .). -4 points.

If you said D, you're making it all too clear that you're out of the loop. If Smith was truly your mentor, he should have clued you in to his imminent departure, as well as to his future plans. This tactic exposes your attachment to someone who didn't keep you informed (see Pin the Tail on the Donkey). 0 points.

The correct answer is A. Stall. This lets you figure out a strategy appropriate for the situation, which in this case might be to do a little reconnaissance work, then call back and continue the conversation by offering, "Listen, now that things are really shaking up, how can I help?" In other words, take the high ground and imply that the news is somehow good for you. This isn't true, but it's the last thing your enemy wants to hear, so you get credit for that alone. 4 points.

2. For the last five years you and your colleague/rival Crystal have worked for Blake, an executive vice president with a wife and kids. Blake has been a judicious manager, dividing his attention equally between the two of you.

But a few weeks ago Blake and Crystal went off on a business trip, and when they returned it was clear that more than business had taken place while they were away. Crystal now spends an hour behind Blake's closed door every day, and when they emerge, they're glowing in that way that only lovers do.

Do you . . .

A. Hide for the next year and a half?

B. Call the company's ethics hot line and report the couple?

C. Take advantage of this opportunity to have your own affair, knowing that no one will be paying any attention to you?

D. Resolve to work twice as hard to compensate for your rival's new edge?

Answers:

If you chose B, you may suffer. Few people who report ethics violations remain truly anonymous (see Zipper Problems II). And if others find out that you're a squealer, your reputation may never recover. 0 points.

Choosing C may only land you an unhappy office relationship, as well as big trouble. And if you're too obvious about it, your peers, who can't touch Crystal, will happily spread the news of your affair. -4 points.

I wish it weren't so, but D probably won't get you anywhere. Hard work seldom makes up the difference in your respective statuses. Blake wants to believe in Crystal and everything she says. No amount of work will make up for Crystal's casual critiques of you. 1 point.

The correct choice is A. Sex usually works only in the short term (see Zipper Problems I). If you can manage to hang in there for about eighteen months, unless Blake and Crystal fall in love (in which case, if they're smart, one of them will leave the company), their affair will evaporate, as will Crystal's edge. 4 points.

3. You've just started working for a new boss, Jason, who's smart but overworked. Three days into the job Jason comes into your office waving a sheaf of papers he prepared with other members of his team, whom you haven't yet met. The papers, which are critical to your department's survival, form the basis of Jason's recommendation to the board that your firm open its next micromanufacturing plant in Micronesia.

The report isn't very good, but it's salvageable. Before you've had time to think through your response, Jason's back in your office. He asks, eagerly, "What do you think?"

You answer:

A. "Jason, I think the people supporting you have let you down. But I'm confident I can whip this back into shape if you can give me an extra few days."

B. "Fabulous! You did an incredible job."

C. "The way you handled the potential capital issues was really savvy—possibly the best I've ever seen in my life. But other parts are a little soft, and maybe we can talk about that later."

D. "Let me get back to you soon."—i.e.: Delay him, then talk to your colleagues about how to fix the report.

Answers:

If you chose A, you're looking to make enemies. Jason will tell the others what you think of their work, as well as his. Don't start your new job with an insult. -4 points.

B is an example of pure ass-kissing. Kissing ass serves no function other than to convince anyone who overhears you that you're a toad. This gets you nowhere. O points.

If you chose D, and you plan to go around the office plotting with your colleagues, you're only going to make Jason paranoid when he finds out, as he inevitably will. -4 points.

Sucking up, C, is the best response. There's an important difference between kissing ass and sucking up (see How to Suck Up). Kissing ass insults everyone's intelligence. But when you suck up, you zero in on what's good about your boss's work and emphasize it, making him feel better about himself. Now you're on the right track to improving the report, which you do need to do. 4 points.

KEY

12 or above: Either you're brilliant, you can't add, or you cheated. If the latter is true, you need serious guidance.

9–11: For the most part, you're getting it right. People approach you for advice. But think how much easier your life would be if you would just give this book to your co-workers instead of spending time coaching them.

5–8: You have a clue about what's going on, but you rarely put it all together. You need this book. Read it carefully. Take notes.

Below 5: You're actively bad at politics. Carry this book with you at all times, taking care to turn the jacket inside out so that no one knows what you're really reading.

WORK
WOULD BE
GREAT

IF IT WEREN'T FOR THE PEOPLE

This Could Be the Start of Something Big

*(The New Job, the New Friend,
the New Company, the New Lover . . .)*

A NEW KID IN TOWN

PIN THE TAIL ON THE DONKEY

POLITICS IN THE TIME OF CHOLERA

YOU'VE GOT TO HAVE FRIENDS

ZIPPER PROBLEMS I

ZIPPER PROBLEMS II

A NEW KID IN TOWN

The moment someone new and important arrives in the office, everyone else scrambles for information and the grapevine launches into hyperdrive. Although the talk is loud and varied, it tends to consist of a few basic themes: Is this new person to be reckoned with? Is this person going to threaten me? Is this a person of any consequence at all?

Often people think it's easy to pick winners. They assume they're the ones who sport the basic, traditional Top Guy look. If it's a woman, she'll have perfectly coiffed hair, perfectly matched accessories, and a wrinkle-free Armani suit. If it's a guy, he'll be wearing a white-collared blue shirt with tastefully sized initials on the cuffs and a moderately hip tie.

Don't judge a boss by his or her collar. Images are deceiving. Instead, wait. People think they have to declare their allegiance to a new leader quickly. It's not so: You can stay in neutral for a long time. Once you've declared yourself, it's hard to undeclare, so be very careful—missing the mark can be expensive.

For instance: One Seattle bank recruited Lucia, an executive vice president from a Boston-based concern; since no one knew anything about her, the first day Lucia arrived everyone was watching her like a hawk. One young man in particular practically attached himself surgically to Lucia, and for the rest of the week he made sure that everyone else knew he'd found a powerful protector, even trying out the occasional "We think . . ." regarding various items on the firm's agenda.

A week later, however, Lucia decided the new job was a fiasco, and she was on the next plane back to Boston, leaving the young man not only mentorless, but suffering from such a complete loss of face that he was virtually faceless. Everyone knew his story, and it was basically the only story about him they knew. Bottom line: Young Man never recovered. He was gone six months later.

In other words: Don't jump on the new arrival's bandwagon until you know the entire score. If that process takes months, so be it. The others who have jumped in ahead of you are risking their career lives. If the new person really is good, he'll notice your prudence, and you may end up getting rewarded anyway.

And what do you do when you're the new kid in town?

Your first few weeks are more about data collection than task completion: who's who, what's going on, where the action takes place, when to make a move, how things get done. To discover all this, you should meet as many people as possible. Don't settle into any patterns. If you have lunch with Benjie the first day, say no if he asks you the second day. You can't take the risk of being associated with him if it turns out he's a political pariah. (Also notice that Benjie asked you two days in a row—which could mean any number of things, some positive, some negative—and file it away for future use.)

Invariably, on the first day of a job, someone will approach you offering friendship. **Beware the first person who wants to be your friend.** The odds are there's a good reason for this and that it's generally not good for you.

Also: Say as little as possible. Unless you've been brought in with a clear mandate to shake things up, for at least six months tell people that, whatever it is they've been doing, they've been doing it well. And, while they're still unsure if they should be threatened by you, get them to tell you as much as possible.

In the beginning you won't understand the landscape. Maybe your boss is locked in a tough political struggle. Maybe she's on her way out. (If she were on her way up, you'd probably know by now, because she would have alluded to it in your job interviews: "There's a lot of opportunity here for someone like you," she'd have said, "and maybe by next year, if you play your cards right . . .")

One quick way to determine your boss's situation is to pay attention to how others respond to Boss's name. "Hi," you say. "I work for Elizabeth." Listen to the response and pay particular attention if it's noncommittal. You can also get a sense of your boss's power from the speed with which others react to your requests. "I'm Kenneth, and I've just started here in Elizabeth's area," you say. "I need a computer setup." Is the answer, "We can do it four weeks from Thursday," or "Right away"?

Tip: Ask questions. Say to your boss: "Whose help do I need in order to accomplish my work?" And don't forget, "Big Fella, is there anyone you'd like me to meet to make things easier for you?" Position yourself as someone who wants to get things done and who knows how to work on a team. "I need to know what's important," you say, "and how I can help you move it forward." Couch your questions in terms of the goals in your department and the ways in which you can facilitate their completion.

Final tip: Don't play power games your first week. Example: Architect Millie took a new job at a large outfit in another city, where, on her first day, she met Philip, the office manager. Millie was having trouble with her phone, and so he got on the case pronto and thought he'd fixed it. The following morning his phone rang. "My goddamn phone isn't working right," Millie was screaming. "Fix it now!"

Because Philip was the guy who could make everyone else's life easier, he was a company favorite. Word spread about Millie long before she ever had a dial tone.

↪ The Evil Twin on new arrivals: I once fell victim to someone's Evil Twin when I switched jobs. My new peer and associate, Oliver, had far more experience than I had, but he'd been warned by his superiors not to go after me or he'd get hurt, too. This warning had the same effect on Oliver that similar ones had on my older brother when we were little— Oliver simply learned not to hurt me in public or any place it showed.

Oliver's goal was to keep his own position strong and undermine me, his competition. So his Evil Twin strategy was to offer me endless advice, some of it useful but much of it specifically designed to land me in trouble. The genius was that the real advice was always grounded in stuff that was concrete and checkable—"Everyone gets in early here, so if you arrive after eight A.M., you'll look like a slug." The rest of it was pure misinformation—"The guys in sales don't like local advertising"—which took me a great deal of time to sort out. This is a classic Evil Twin ploy, and one that often succeeds.

Luckily, someone took pity on me and explained the local rules vis-a-vis being picked on: Pick back. So I went after Oliver on a petty matter, but I did it with such ferocity that he understood that I was willing to take him on, and as soon as he knew that he backed off.

PIN THE TAIL ON THE DONKEY

There once was a time when, at the start of your career, you'd attach yourself to a superior who could, in turn, guarantee you job security. And if your mentor left the organization, you went along, too—particularly if you worked on Wall Street, where your contacts often counted for more than your talent.

Mentors are no longer as viable—today's competitive environment is far too tough. Few people spend their careers at one place, and it generally takes years to make the right connection with the right person. You can't just walk into a company and decide on the basis of a fast compliment or a nice conversation that you're willing to attach your career to someone else's, no matter how powerful or ambitious this person seems. You have to know his or her strengths and weaknesses, and that takes time.

Yet people keep trying to pin their careers to another's—most often when they're afraid they don't have the talent to succeed alone. It's a risky idea. Major hazard: **Donkey's gone, you're gone.** If your mentor doesn't make it, you may be so attached to him that when he's fired you no longer fit inside the organization.

And there's no reason to believe that he can or will take you to the next job. Unless you know this person extremely well, you have no way of telling whether your loyalty will be returned. You could easily be attaching yourself to a user. Now, that can be a happy, symbiotic relationship if you're a user, too, but at least you ought to know what you're getting into.

Tip: If you're a woman and you've pinned your tail to a male donkey, be prepared: Everyone will think you're having an affair with him. It doesn't have to be true for people to speculate. In fact, it's often easier for people to speculate when it *isn't* true, because you're more relaxed and warm with each other in public than you would be if something was actually underfoot.

⟶ The Evil Twin on picking mentors: Normally, in these kinds of symbiotic relationships, the two of you share the applause. You get some, he gets some, and the priority is working it out pleasantly.

But when you're ready to fight with your donkey, it's time to let your Evil Twin step up and demand the spotlight. For instance: One donkey I knew, George, took a vacation just before a big presentation was coming up. The moment George left, Lennie, his protégé, decided to go after his job, and worked maniacally on the presentation while George was gone. And by the time George returned, the spotlight shone only on Len and George was obsolete. Now Len is someone else's donkey.

Tip for donkeys: Nothing brings out the Evil Twin faster than a junior person's ambition. They don't mean it; they just can't help it. It's like adolescence. So when your protégé smiles radiantly at you, remember, this too shall pass. Someday that beam may hide a secret plan to take your job away.

Evil Twin counterattack: If you see your protégé going for the brass ring, don't fight for it—openly. Instead, position yourself as the sponsor of this great young talent. Act like a proud parent; pretend you encouraged him to step into the light, indirectly claiming full responsibility for his emergence. "Isn't Len cute," you coo. "Look at him go. My little baby boy, who would have thought it?" If you're lucky, and you're a good actor, you can convince others that you've been in complete control of the situation the entire time.

POLITICS IN THE TIME OF CHOLERA

As in nature, every now and then some force will appear from out of the blue and change the landscape of your office: new management teams, hostile takeovers, mergers, and so on. During these times a surge in office political maneuvering occurs, all the rules change, and if you're not careful, you can get caught in huge political tsunamis.

Every move made by every player in the company is now cause for concern and open to interpretation and speculation.

Remember: The office is holistic. It operates as a single organism rather than as a collection of individual, unrelated parts. A new boss on the 104th floor can make enough waves that the man working in Records Management in the subbasement drowns as a result.

You never have to pay more attention than during times of flux. If you're reading this book carefully, you're already training for these moments, because they demand your best political response for every situation. And since the odds are good that you'll hit one or more of these waves in your career, you need to establish your habits before they hit. It's like boarding a luxury liner: As soon as you arrive, the crew takes you through the emergency drill. Learn the drill at the office, too.

The reason you need to remain firmly in control of yourself is that no one else will be. You'll witness every kind of acting out imaginable. Whatever your colleagues usually do, their behavior under stress will make them do more of it. They'll make more friends, they'll make more enemies, and they'll have more problems with zippers unzipping when they shouldn't. The drinkers will drink more, the nervous babblers will babble more, the eaters will grow bigger. You'll see everyone's worst side, including your own.

Here's the upside: These are the times when you can rise to the top, when you can vault a couple of levels of responsibility. Anything can happen in a crisis. Whatever was fixed comes unfixed. Whatever was in boxes or in little cubes falls out. And once everything's loose, you can move much more rapidly than under normal, orderly, constrained conditions.

Caution: **Don't make friends with the company's enemies in bad times.** You'll probably be courted by someone representing interests hostile to your company, such as the media or a competitor. Why shouldn't they come to you? You're valuable to them as an insider, and you'll be presented with seemingly excellent reasons to align your interests with theirs.

Basically, these enemies offer you two choices: revenge for all the petty injustices you've endured, or the chance to leverage your way off a sinking ship onto a winning team. However, if you're still accepting your company's paycheck, show some loyalty. And from a practical point of view, if you're so deceitful that you'd try to hurt a company whose money you're taking, why should anyone ever trust you again? It's like marrying someone who sneaked out on his first spouse to go out with you—it opens the door to doubt.

⬧ The Evil Twin on vast change: Since the stress of upheaval guarantees that everyone will be on their worst behavior, if you're so determined, it also guarantees the best opportunity to take people out. You know how your enemies will act under pressure because you know their weaknesses will be exponentially increased. Therefore, it's a perfect time, and a perfectly dangerous time, to sow seeds of insecurity. With a little extra gasoline on their own fires of doubt, your rivals are likely to self-immolate.

For instance, here's a scene a friend engineered at a large public relations firm that had been taken over by a still-larger competitor. Julia and Winston were rivals in a department that was about to feel all the changes directly. Both employees were completely at sea, but Julia decided to let her Evil Twin grab the rudder.

Winston came from the old boys' school, whose methods had

played well at their firm, since most of the staff had gone to similar schools and lived in similar suburbs. These guys talked the same talk and walked the same walk, and it had been a little tough for those who didn't speak their language (see Speaking in Tongues), including Julia, who always felt excluded from the club.

The new firm operated differently; several women held senior management positions. Julia had been watching Winston closely enough to note that one manifestation of his uneasiness was a tendency to talk the ol' boy talk even more than usual, particularly to her.

The very day the new company took over, she called him. "Hi," she said. "Hey, babe," Winston answered in his most sexually nuanced voice, and continued in that tone for almost a full minute. Unfortunately for Winston, Julia was with the new big-deal vice president at the time, on the speaker phone, in front of a cast of thousands. The new people never got over their perception of Winston as a sex-crazed maniac, and the new women seemed reluctant to enter an elevator alone with him.

Also evil: New players will appear in situations of turmoil. Use them. Your enemies will feel more insecure if you appear to be developing an alliance with the new people, and that can drive them crazy enough to do stupid things. Make them overestimate your ties. Allow them to overhear that you and the new man Tony were having drinks last night. Let them see Tony's phone messages. Tell them about Tony's children.

The slickest version of this I've ever seen had the Evil Twin downplaying the connection while his familiar, the dedicated assistant, performed her own rendition of Paul Revere's ride through the office, announcing to person after person, "I can't believe how often that new guy Tony calls my boss."

YOU'VE GOT TO HAVE FRIENDS...

Except at the office, where you seldom have real friends.

You may think that you've just established a great connection with a great new friend. But you haven't. **Friends are what you have outside the office.** Inside you can have cordial relations, nice lunches, long conversations, and good buddies, but that's it.

It's hard to cement a friendship when you have so many other agendas. You might be peers, in which case you're both competing for money, position, or perks such as the company seats at baseball games. Or one of you is higher up on the totem pole, in which case you're constantly made aware of that fact by everyone else in the organization, as well as by the extra money and power one of you wields. Sooner or later the weight of the imbalance causes the friendship to collapse.

Perhaps this sounds cynical, but if you don't believe me, you're either a poor judge of people or the company where you're working is in trouble—because if all your friends work in your office, things are much too cozy, which means that you're all insulated from the rough-and-tumble of the highly competitive marketplace.

It's not until you leave your office that you discover who your friends are. After I left my first job I was startled to realize how many people who'd been part of my daily life were suddenly absent from it. I thought I'd done something wrong, but I soon discovered this was just the way it is: When you leave your job, you leave behind your desk, your computer, your letterhead, and most of your buddies.

At the office, work comes before friendships. Anyone who approaches you and says, "But I thought we were friends" is likely to be protesting because of some other agenda. Work is about power, and power corrodes any consensual relationship, including friendship.

Tip: **Trust everyone and no one.** Don't be so paranoid about keeping secrets that you don't talk to a soul, but do make it a point to learn exactly what you can trust specific people to do. Some people can give you reliable feedback. You may even find someone who knows how to keep a confidence. But being able to trust a friend with a real secret is a rare treat. Even the IRA discovered a double agent in its ranks.

Case in point: A few years ago, Jay and Nick, two partners at an Oregon high-tech firm, were going through a rough breakup. The ferocity of their professional divorce was as intense as their former friendship. Each felt he had carried the company, and each was angry.

One afternoon they had lunch to discuss the split. "You should know that subjects we'd rather not talk about with each other are going to have to be raised," Jay said. "So let's let the lawyers handle those things."

"Like what?" Nick asked.

"You know," said Jay. He hemmed and hawed and finally admitted that he had told his lawyer about Nick's frequent sexual liaisons with their assistant.

Nick paused, then said, "Evidently your lawyer doesn't know about your massage parlor habit, does she? But then again, neither does your wife."

Within hours, years of confidences were spilling out to a variety of interested parties, including competitors and lawyers. You just never know when even your best friend is going to decide that, hey, you were never really that close.

Executives in exile: Sometimes the people you like the most are taken out in the middle of your burgeoning mutual love fest. What do you do now that they're gone?

Most people who leave a company unwillingly have only bad things to say about it. It isn't going to help your own relationship to the workplace to hear a friend drone on and on about what a miserable hellhole you're in. You don't want that negative energy—but your friend needs to say these things as she goes through her own stages of grief.

Nor do you want her to visit you at the office. Even though you're only being loyal to a friend, you'll look disloyal to your paycheck.

So provide your ex-co-workers with structured support away from the office. Don't flaunt your friendships with them at work. And don't share indiscretions about the office. Just say, "I still have to work there." After about six months, when they've worked through their anger, or bitterness, or grief, you can resume your friendship, which will thrive if and only if you can find something other than the office to talk about. If you can't, you probably never were friends.

—⚡ The Evil Twin on friends: People think they're using their Evil Twins when they fake friendships with others, but it's not so. Pretending to like someone isn't Evil Twin. It's dumb. You play tennis with the regional manager even though you secretly despise her; you go shopping with the head of Marketing although you find him a jerk. Wrong. **Don't pretend to be friends with anyone.**

The problem is that you're being obvious, and obvious doesn't work—that's why it's called "obvious." The regional manager doesn't want to look as though she's been fooled by your blatant advances, so after she promotes your rival, and you whine, "But I thought we were friends," you'll quickly discover that she knew better. You should, too.

What's the correct course of action when someone tries faking a friendship with you? That's when you use your Evil Twin legitimately. Pretend you believe him. In the process of faking it, your false friend may well reveal something useful. And, of course, you're the one calling the ultimate shots, because while he thinks he's pulling the wool over your eyes, the truth is that you can see right through it.

Many years ago I worked at a place where Ian, a good-looking and ambitious young man, was known for his charm. Some fell for it, some didn't. I didn't. And for the most part, he left me alone—until I got promoted into an area that Ian felt represented his future.

Not long after my announcement, Ian found a way for us to work on a small project. "Ronna," he oozed, "I can't tell you how happy I am for you. Let's lunch." And from that moment on, Ian showered me with his considerable charm.

Not for one second did I believe that Ian had suddenly awoken to my own magic. Not for one second did I think this sudden show of friendliness represented anything other than Ian's own agenda. But although I wasn't interested in Ian, my Evil Twin was. Why not? Ian, through his endless manipulation of the office, tended to know more than anyone. There was no question that I could use that information.

So every now and then Ian and I had lunch. I never told him anything that I didn't want spread through his vast network, and I learned plenty of things that I wouldn't have otherwise. And I even came to admire the man's relentless ambition—since, unlike everything else about him, it was genuine.

ZIPPER PROBLEMS I

A few years ago government regulators were pounding on Prudential Securities for decade-old marketing irregularities, and the scrutiny came at a point when I'd just inherited the job of running crisis management, which meant that I was on call for many late-night traumas. It wasn't easy.

One evening—after many other equally difficult nights—I was sitting in my office with two outside attorneys, sweating, nervous, stressed out, waiting for the phone to ring. What was I thinking? Not just that my eighteen thousand colleagues would suffer terribly if things went wrong. I was also thinking that one of those lawyers had the most beautifully shaped upper lip I'd ever seen. I wanted to touch it. Even the other man, who a few hours earlier had struck me as eerily apelike, was looking attractive in a hairy way.

Then we got the phone call, and the situation wasn't so bad after all. Now, when I looked at the second man, he was simply simian again, and the other's beautiful upper lip had faded from the top of my mind to a pleasant memory.

It's the same as in all those war stories: Pressure can, and often does, make for sexual tension. **Sexual energy in the office is inevitable.** It happens all around you, in places you can see and in places you can't.

Another of my jobs at Prudential included working with counsel to fix what we called "zipper problems"—as in zippers that weren't zipped when they should have been, which generally involved older men with power behaving badly with younger women who didn't have power but who had looks. And, less often—but with more frequency in the '90s than in the '80s—older women with power and younger men with looks. And occasionally men and men, women and women, or one man and two women, and so on. Basically, whatever sexual realities exist in the outside world exist inside the office as well.

What I learned from all this: **The best way to deal with sex at the office is to manage your own sexual response.**

To do that, recognize that you can, and you will, have these responses. I agree with former president Jimmy Carter's comments about feeling lust in his heart. It's perfectly okay to look. No amount of political correctness can legislate away the fact that people are drawn to each other, whether they're at the gym, at the beach, or in the elevator.

But you can't touch. Follow this advice and you'll avoid trouble. It's that simple.

The other side of the issue: What happens when you're suddenly the target of someone else's interest?

Allan was an upper-level executive with whom I worked nicely for a year until, out of the blue, he developed a completely absurd, out-of-control crush on me. This can happen anywhere to anyone, even me. So whenever I take a new position, I also take a few precautionary steps.

For instance, I quickly introduce my husband around the office and talk about him frequently. That doesn't stop the nosing around, but it's a kind of territorial marking that indicates a lack of interest on my part, and it makes most men more comfortable around me.

My system's not foolproof, however, and it had no effect on Allan at all. As is often the case with office crushes, Allan's behavior was irrational.

Still, I managed to handle him, making sure that the two of us were seldom alone, and never with the door shut. Then, without warning, Allan selected me for a special, high-visibility assignment that no one would have considered giving me without his recommendation.

Here's the political side: I got the offer in part for the wrong reasons, but I accepted anyway. Allan had chosen me so we could spend time together. But, I rationalized, plenty of bad things had already happened to me because of my gender. Why not accept some of the good things, too? I was careful not to lead Allan on. I had never in any way indicated to him that I was a willing conspirator. My conscience was clean.

When it comes to your own sex appeal, establish standards about using the power you acquire when someone decides he or she likes you. Without standards, you can land in some serious trouble. But there's no hard-and-firm law that says you can't take advantage of a situation. You have to negotiate with yourself to find the place where you're comfortable—and make sure it's one that won't come back to haunt you.

Since I never crossed the line with Allan, the worst accusation someone could have made was "You got that job because Allan had the hots for you." This I could either shrug off, or say "Me? Ridiculous!" The important thing was that I could sleep at night—without Allan.

Tip: What's the best strategy for fending off an advance? **Don't let it get to the order.** When you're talking to a salesman, at the point during the pitch when he thinks he's got you, he'll say, "So I'll put you down for one hundred of these babies, right?" You need to do your best to stop your admirer from getting to the order, which, in the case of zippers, is usually, "So, like, you wanna go have a drink or something?"

The Evil Twin on sex in, around, or near the office: Sex wakes up everyone's Evil Twin. That's because sex is irrational, disruptive, and creates winners and losers, especially when people use their sexual Evil Twins to get what they want.

The major problem with sex: It only works in the short term. After about eighteen months, the affair will probably end (unless it turns into love, in which case you move in together, and one of you will probably have to change jobs). So if you want to use sex to advance, figure that you'd better get what you want within a year and a half, or else.

But you still probably won't get it. Texas football coach Darrell Royal once said that when you throw a forward pass there are three things that can happen, and two of them are bad. It's even worse with office sex—there are many, many more bad endings than happy ones. You get tired of him/her, he/she gets tired of you, Boss's spouse finds out, your spouse finds out, Lover goes to another company, Lover's boss finds out and fires you instead of Lover. And so on. It's a time-bound strategy that will take you only so far.

Anyway, you have to be very cold to do it well. You can't care that Lover won't leave the spouse, or that you'll have to lead your social life without Lover, or that other people will look at you with suspicion. It's almost a career in itself. I've always thought it's easier just to do your job.

A particularly effective Evil Twin strategy: Diane, an attractive banker, went on a business trip with her married boss, Sam, who was widely known for his extracurricular activity. So everyone assumed Diane and Sam would have an affair, too. Diane was smarter than that. When she returned from the trip, she called all her friends, along with her enemies, and insisted that she was *not* sleeping with Sammy. Her friends and enemies alike all wondered why Diane was protesting so much—she really must have had the affair, they guessed, or she wouldn't be so eager to correct everyone's assumption. Within a few days the word spread that Diane and Sam were an item.

Actually, nothing had happened on the trip. Diane had used all her wiles to keep herself free of any attachment with Sam, but got everyone else to treat her as though they had a special relationship.

ZIPPER PROBLEMS II

Sometimes the most pressing sexual issues at the office involve other people's sex drives.

For instance, let's say that you and Cyndy are vying for your boss's attention when, from out of left field, the boss decides that Cyndy is one highly attractive woman. Flattered, Cyndy sheds her common sense and starts having an affair with the Big Guy. How can you compete with her now?

For now, you can't.

Even if you're doing everything right, you're going to lose out to the person who's having sex with the boss. **In other words, a blow job always beats a good job.**

It's not only that the boss loves Cyndy, or thinks he does. That's not important. It's the little cuts that kill you. Cyndy now has, among other things, the boss's ear. How can you possibly counter Cyndy's casual asides, such as "Oh, you know, I don't think Pat likes you." Or "Pat just doesn't seem to be a part of the team."

Well, if you're Pat, you've had it. The boss has to trust Cyndy, and now he doesn't trust you.

What are your options? One is to deal with it like a baby: Complain, whine, and moan. This will work about as well as it did when you were a child trying to get an ice-cream cone before you ate your dinner. Bad choice.

The other, more mature (and therefore less appealing) option: Be realistic. You can only win against a sexual relationship if you can hang on long enough, since an affair's duration is usually the aforementioned eighteen months. After that, it's over except for the recriminations and the betrayals. If you can find a way to get out of town, or stall for eighteen months, do it.

—✧ The Evil Twin on other people's zippers: You can always try to get the offending couple fired. Nearly every large corporation has a personnel office and, perhaps, an ethics hot line. If and only if you can get away with remaining anonymous, consider reporting them.

But I can tell you from experience that practically no one manages to remain anonymous. When I supervised an ethics hot line, I knew for a fact that everyone in our official chain kept their mouths shut. And still people often found out who had told what to whom.

Why? **Snitching is like planning the perfect murder: It's hard to pull off.** Someone overhears your phone call, someone watches you watching them, or, most frequently, you brag about what you did. You confide in one person, that person confides in someone else—it's too juicy a secret to keep—and soon everyone knows. And even if everyone else was suffering because of the affair, and they're secretly glad that you made the call, they still won't forget that you were the one who picked up the phone.

The Way You Do the Things You Do

(Handling the Money, the Memos, the Truth, the Clock . . .)

BEING THERE

What does it matter? You come to a meeting looking like a million bucks, you're the boss's favorite, you're filled with schemes that can make you and everyone around you a fortune. What does it matter if you're a half an hour late?

A lot. **Even if you're doing everything else right, if you're doing time wrong, you're toast.** Mishandling time is one of the dumbest political moves people make—people who are otherwise smart, aggressive, capable. If you make it a habit to show up late, that's the beginning and the end of how your associates will define you.

The way people handle time says everything. For instance, when a meeting begins, observe the hierarchy of who arrives when. If John, who's compulsively late, now appears before anyone else, something's up. If Marcia, who's normally prompt, starts showing up late with a limp apology, there's been a shift in power somewhere.

Because you could always be doing something else, the decision to be on time tells the others at the meeting what you think of them. Therefore, at a general meeting, junior people mill around beforehand, as do those who openly want something, such as salespeople.

Another sign of power involves how much of the meeting has to restart when late arrivals appear. Junior people don't get as much as a nod, the implied message being "Catch up yourself." On the other hand, if you show up late and everyone's not only embarrassed they started but they recapitulate all that's transpired, you're probably sitting in a power spot.

The bottom line: Time is of the essence. Don't mess with it. But since the culture of time varies from company to company, scope out how others are behaving and meld into the crowd. At some places, where no one's ever tardy, five minutes can be a big deal. Elsewhere, showing up five minutes late would translate into waiting fifty-five minutes instead of an hour.

No matter what your personal predisposition, live by your company's clock while you're at work. Someone once said that the best epitaph a corporate executive could have on his tombstone is: "He was predictable." That's what you want to be, time-wise.

You also need to learn quickly about "face time"—the hours when the Powers That Be need to see your face. In some design firms rolling in at around noon is acceptable behavior, while at a bank it might be grounds for dismissal. Likewise, at some places, staying late at night can win you bonus points; at others, it's a sign you're mismanaging your workload.

Companies' unspoken policies also vary regarding what constitutes a good excuse for an absence. There's a famous story about an up-and-coming young executive at a Major Chicago Company who wasn't quite on track. One late afternoon, during an extended meeting, he announced to his peers that he had to leave because he'd promised his son he'd watch him play Little League. "Now we know your priorities," someone snickered. The company CEO countered: "Yes, and they're darn good ones." This was a breakthrough for the young executive, who, with a little help from his new friend, eventually went on to become CEO himself. At another company, however, he might have been taken out.

⟶ The Evil Twin on time: Let's say your company has a project integral to its success, and therefore to yours as well. Much of the work has been turned over to you, but unfortunately, your boss has also handed some responsibility to Judd, a co worker you think is in over his head.

Use his time habits against him. If you know that Judd's always late in the mornings, schedule important meetings for 8 A.M. He may make the first few, but after that, unless he's really adaptable, he'll revert to his usual tardiness. Eventually everyone else will be so annoyed they'll shut poor Judd out of the project without your having to say a word.

DON'T SWING AT EVERY PITCH

No matter the size of your office or the size of your paycheck, small skirmishes will be taking place all around you at all times during your career. That's not important. What is important: **Don't participate in every battle.**

Take the time to calibrate each one to see if it's worth taking on. The ultimate goal is to engage in as few skirmishes as possible.

For most people, fighting concerns vanity. You'd like to think that you're fighting for some Larger Cause, but you're probably fighting for the cause known as You. These personal fights are the least worthy. Differentiate between your ego and your business—it will save you endless trauma.

When is it right to fight? When you're convinced it's for the long-term good of the company. If you're fighting for your company, and you're in the right job, then your fight should be for your own good, too, even if it takes a while for those interests to line up.

If you can't find a win for the organization that's also right for you, then you're in the wrong place. Leave before they dump you.

That's not easy advice. In fact, following it is one of the toughest things I ever did. Not long ago Prudential recruited Taylor, a new head honcho for marketing. He believed that the company advertising should be focused on the brand level—that is, for the entire corporation. Meanwhile, I was a rallying point for those who believed in advertising each Prudential business separately. So I started to fight, until I realized that, in the long run, the centralization theme might actually be best for the company. So instead of fighting for my turf, I told Taylor that if he genuinely represented the company's new direction, he should ax my budget.

Everyone flipped; offering up a budget is tantamount to human sacrifice. But the bottom line was that my willingness to subordinate my needs to the company's ended up making it possible for me to restructure my career. I can't pretend that throughout these maneuvers I was supremely confident that by losing I would win, but somehow I managed to hold on to the notion that if it was truly right for the company it was right for me, too. And it was.

Bear in mind: If, after eliminating all the petty fights on the horizon, you still see a large number of battles looming, consider two options: (1) therapy—for there's a good chance your vision is blurry; or (2) a new job. Any position that demands that you fight every day is probably one you can afford to lose.

—⟲ The Evil Twin on fights: If you've pinpointed a rival at your organization as someone who swings at every pitch, and you foresee a major power struggle in the near future, take advantage of his propensity to fight by subtly pushing him into every petty battle. By the time the Big One rolls around, either he'll be too tired to put up his dukes or he'll have exhausted his credibility, rendering himself unable to fight you successfully.

For instance, my friend Calvin once worked with a man whose office nickname was Make-My-Day. The man was a walking, talking imitation of Dirty Harry (if you excuse the fact that he was at least half a foot shorter and wore Coke bottle glasses). Make-My-Day was a natural-born fighter. He fought high, he fought low; where he found that energy to fight all day, no one knows. All Calvin knew was that Make-My-Day had been assigned to his team, and Calvin's team was noted for its remarkable ability to cooperate.

Calvin decided that the only possible tactic was to take out Make-My-Day. And since Calvin was known for his total disinterest in politics, he was the most dangerous kind of player. So when Make-My-Day first reported to Calvin, Calvin immediately entangled him in a small but brutal fight about whether Make-My-Day could have a better cubicle. Then he lured him into a battle about whether he could bring his old assistant with him. And so on: Make-My-Day's new hours, an alleged new dress code, the number of personal phone calls he could make. By the time Calvin was finished with Make-My-Day, the battle-weary man had trudged off to Calvin's boss to report that he could never get along with someone as ornery as Calvin, and he demanded to be transferred.

Calvin's boss was startled. No one had ever called Calvin anything but a pussycat. But since he liked Calvin and didn't want to make trouble, he agreed to the transfer. Make-My-Day was yesterday's news.

FEEDING THE HAND
THAT BITES YOU

Just before his flameout, Graham was looking like a guy with a big future. The midsize Dallas accounting firm where he worked was about to be acquired by a giant one, and because Graham was well liked and hardworking, it seemed obvious that his career had meteoric potential.

But, as is often the case, Graham was insecure, and company acquisitions make for those times that fire the soft clay of insecurity into the brittleness of self-destruction (see Politics in the Time of Cholera). Graham had no reason to worry, but he wasn't thinking smart; he was thinking scared. Did he really have a good reputation? Yes, but he was afraid he didn't. Did he really need more firepower behind him? No, he was already well positioned. Were there lots of unknowns? Yes, but the unknown isn't always negative. Those three-in-the-morning voices of doom were drowning out Graham's common sense.

As his fear of the upcoming acquisition grew, so did his agitation. Graham's specialty was auditing, and he figured he'd soon be warring with the Big Company's own auditors for position and power. He also figured that he'd lose, since they were a known commodity and he was new. So he decided that, rather than wait for what he thought was the inevitable ax, he'd be better off taking the offensive.

A few years earlier, the Big Company's internal accounting

department had tinkered with some accounting records, creating an
unpleasant situation few people knew about. But Graham was among
them, since his old assistant now worked there and kept in touch.
Graham also had a friend who worked at an industry newspaper.
After intense brooding, Graham leaked the Big Company's indiscretions to his journalist friend so that his new rivals would look bad in
the press.

At first the plan worked—the story appeared, and the internal
accountants were scrambling to justify their actions. No one knew
Graham's role in all this. But the scheme gained momentum when
the story moved from trade papers to the general business press, and
now the Big Company had big problems. The upshot: Big Company
got distracted, and the acquisition fizzled.

Although no one could ever prove it, a few people at Graham's
company noticed that Graham had both a former assistant at the Big
Company as well as an old friend at the Industry Rag—and they wondered. Some of them even wondered aloud, which made even more
people wonder just how far Graham would go to get what he wanted.

There are going to be times when you'll be tempted to influence
your career by venturing outside your company. Nearly everyone has
a friend who works for an industry watchdog, or a trade association,
or the press. Maybe you think, "I gotta tell someone about this." Or
"They can't get away with that. I'm calling *60 Minutes.*"

But consider the options. Is this really the way to go? Let's say
you've decided to advance your career by giving an outsider information about your company. The problem is that now you've lost
control. Maybe, as in Graham's case, the situation is worse than an-
ticipated and you're opening up a can of worms. Or maybe you're not
as subtle as you think and it becomes public knowledge that you're
the leak. Even if they can't prove it, they'll still never look at you in
the same way—or trust you again.

It's hard to hurt someone else without hurting yourself. The business press is rife with stories of people who tried to curry favor for themselves by venturing outside the normal channels and who were damaged goods forever after.

Special attention: the media. For many, the media isn't an issue. But an accidental run-in can blindside almost anyone, so here are few essential rules:

1. The media doesn't exist to help you—even if you consider yourself the good guy. Why should the media be different from any other collection of businesspeople? The politics of the media company drives the media company. Maybe someone needs to get promoted. She wants something sensational, so why not blow up a small story into something juicier? Maybe someone wants a Pulitzer Prize to guarantee a raise. He needs something prestigious, and what better than investigative revelations about your company?

2. No matter how much they depend on the media to gather information, most businesspeople, when reading coverage about something they know well, recognize the coverage as naïve, distorted, or just plain wrong. Keep that in mind whenever the media call. **Just because it's in print or on television doesn't mean it's accurate.** Unless the reporter is both gifted and honest, don't be surprised to find your words misconstrued or manipulated on the page.

3. **Don't trust a member of the media any more than you would any other complete stranger.** I know too many people who, once a smart reporter got them on the line, were so flattered by the attention that they forgot all the rules and talked too much.

For the most part, unless your need for self-promotion is so great that containing it would take more energy than you can muster, don't talk to the media unless you have no other choice. Let the professionals do it.

—⚔ The Evil Twin on talking to others: You've noticed that your
rival has a tendency to overinflate her importance. She never misses
a chance to claim an idea. She's the first to say, once a project has
succeeded, that she was its original champion.

If her mouth has been bothering you, redirect it to someone
who can give her something to chew on. The next time a reporter
calls your company, make sure that during the course of his research
he talks to your rival. If her ego is as ripe as you think it is, you'll soon
be seeing her name in print, taking credit for something—an idea, an
achievement, a program—that belongs to someone else. You don't
have to worry about her anymore; now she's got an enemy who's
much angrier than you are. With any luck, it'll be the boss.

HOW TO SUCK UP

I love being sucked up to. Most people do.

I operate on the theory that everyone feels inadequate and, at the same time, that everyone needs to feel good about himself or herself. We all want to be able to say, "I'm important and I'm good" to the mirror, or to our mom, or to anyone else who'll listen. Trying to convince ourselves that we're genuinely okay occupies a great deal of our working—and waking—hours.

Furthermore, the only way most people can perform well is with some external validation. So if you can help people feel good about themselves they'll be motivated to rise to the occasion, and you'll find that every wheel's a little more greased than it was before.

In other words, artful sucking up can actually be a powerful means of getting the job done. And it doesn't necessarily involve obsequious behavior.

Example: For years I'd been quarreling with Walt, a vice president with an even-greater-than-normal desire to be admired. Because of our constant battles, work that should have been done wasn't, while the work that was being done took twice as long to finish since our fights were causing uneasy ripples all the way down the company food chain.

So there we were: I was denying him positive feedback, and he was waiting for positive feedback. We were going nowhere. So one day I thought, "This is ridiculous. I keep wanting to win on the issues, but all I'm actually doing is wasting my time as well as everyone else's. Why don't I just tell Walt he's terrific?"

Walt prided himself on being good at negotiating with outside vendors; consequently, he considered this skill to be the world's most important. "You know, Walt," I said one day, "you're so good at this, I think you could teach me an enormous amount."

The man lit up like a Christmas tree. And I realized that I was the idiot for not having said something sooner. From then on, the proper piece of praise for Walt was all I needed to oil the machinery.

Not only does sucking up help your relationships with peers, it does wonders for the boss. Of all my employees, Glenda made me feel my best, because Glenda took the trouble to learn where I felt my strengths lay, and she complimented me on those areas. It's much easier to believe someone who's flattering the parts of you that you like most. As a result, Glenda and I were a good team. She brought out my best self, and therefore my best work. I was smart enough to understand what she was doing, but I was also human enough to enjoy it.

Always treat people above you as though they were your main clients. Think about it. They are. No one is more important to your career than your boss, and his boss, and so on.

Many people are too tough on their bosses because they're afraid they'll look like sycophants. But there's a difference between sucking up and kissing ass. People who do the latter get stuck with a deservedly bad reputation. They have no opinions of their own—all they do is repeat the Big Guy's. Or they blandly compliment their superiors: "Right on, Stan! You can't lose with that plan!" "You're the one for me, Lee." "Atta boy, you're a genius, Roy." Kissing ass is simply a barrage of scattershot, ill-defined compliments hurled without intelligence or thought.

Good sucking up, however, requires work. You don't just throw compliments at everything in sight. Study your target. Find one positive trait you genuinely admire (which may not always be easy).

Then provide services and support in a way that plays up to that strength. Maybe your boss is excellent at giving advice on other people, and you want more. Say so. "Boss, you were dead-on about Marge: At first she says no to new ideas, but then she reconsiders. Thanks for tipping me off to that."

⟶❖ The Evil Twin on sycophancy: Sucking up can be used against bosses who make it impossible for you to do your job. All you need to do is tell them that they're excelling when you know they're not.

Case in point: Boss is about to hand in a six-month project to the Big Boss. She asks you to take a look at it. It's drivel. "Whoa, Boss," you say. "This is great. You've outdone yourself." Boss turns in project; boss gets burned. (Warning: This must be a project from which you can extricate yourself or you'll go down with her.)

The irony is that many people will believe a compliment even when it's far-fetched, so the odds are good that not only won't your boss turn on you, she may believe that you're the only person who appreciates her true genius.

But be careful. If you attempt this approach and fail, you fail in a very major way.

LEAPFROGGING

Your boss is your boss, and for the most part that's all there is to it. But your boss also has a boss, and occasions will arise when you'll want to jump over one hierarchical level to the next, whether it's to right a perceived injustice or to strike up a casual conversation to make sure the Powers That Be are aware of your existence.

Can you do it? Yes. But you have to finesse it exactly right. For instance: You and your boss have been having a serious policy disagreement, and neither of you knows where the Big Boss stands. "Should we take this further up the line?" you wonder aloud. You can even wonder if you can be present at the discussion.

If your boss says no, then drop it.

If he says he's willing to pursue the matter, but without you, ask if you can work with him on his language so he represents your point of view properly. If his idea of being fair is to say, after presenting his side at length: "And the kid sees it differently, but what does he know?" you're not going to win.

Here's another scenario: Your boss is basically an idiot, and you're dying to remove yourself from her orbit by getting closer to her boss. Tough situation. Some companies have skip-step performance reviews, which means you get a review with the boss's boss and a chance to mouth off—but you still have to be careful. Don't say, "Ronnie's a jerk." Say, "Ronnie is great for what I'm doing now, but I feel I'm not getting what I need to go to the next step."

But let's say you don't have this kind of review, and you want to leap over your boss so you can operate more independently. For instance, you've got the kind of position where you're responsible for bringing projects into the company—but your boss is stopping you from acquiring the ones that make the most sense to you and the company at large. You know that if only her boss could see your projects she'd agree with you.

Should you try it? Here your chances depend on a string of variables, such as: Have you done this before? Are you getting along with your boss and can you afford a little tension? Have other people gotten away with this? Is your boss friendly with her boss? How would your boss respond to what could be felt as a threat to her self-esteem? There isn't a single right answer. Be sensible. Be inventive. Be clever.

One solution I've used in the past is camouflage: Find a way to see the Bigger Boss on an unrelated piece of business and then casually drift over to the issue you want to broach. Don't insult your boss while doing it—the Bigger Boss may interpret this as disloyalty to the company, and therefore to her, too.

Your boss's boss is the one who sets the leapfrogging rules by indicating her willingness to be a receiver. Wittingly or not, if she wants you to come to her, she will signal it.

A final choice is simply to tell your boss that you're going to leapfrog. Make her comfortable by making it generic—you're thinking about your future, you want a better sense of where you fit in with the company. You can even ask your boss to set up an appointment for you—a good boss will do that. Just make sure that you tell your boss the truth about what you're going to talk about. If you lie, you'll lose. **Only desperate people play leapfrog wearing cleats.**

— The Evil Twin on jumping over your boss's head: When dealing with a boss you want to torture—only for the right reasons—use leapfrogging to drive him loopy. But be careful: This is a very high-risk Evil Twin maneuver.

The way to do it: Ask for permission to talk to his boss, and if that doesn't work, try every other approach you can think of to open a line of communication with the Powers That Be above him. When and if you get permission, make it clear to your boss that you've established a relationship up there. Casually drop the Big Guy's name in conversation, mentioning what a great backhand he has, or say that you'd never realized how big that weekend place at the lake is.

Now, you may not quite have that kind of connection, but your boss's suspicions will be sparked, and there's no real way for him ever to know for sure—even if he asks his boss directly and receives a negative. If he's properly paranoid, he may still think that something's going on. In fact, if the Big Boss is denying it, he may take that to mean it's bigger than he ever thought possible.

MEMORANDUM HARVEST

If you don't have anything nice to say, don't write it down in a memo. On the whole, memos are usually a bad idea.

What are the circumstances that bring pens to memo-writing fingers? The most common rationale in committing something to paper is to cover your butt. Laziness and defensiveness are also near the top of the list. It's very rare that a long memo doesn't include some built-in defense.

Too many people write too many memos. They write them to prove that they're busy. You know the type: Her desk is piled with stacks of paper, her briefcase is heavy, she looks like an up-and-comer. Or at least she thinks so.

But every time a memo is sent out, it's one more thing your co-workers have to deal with, one more piece of paper in an in-box that needs attention. And so, unless it somehow helps them, it's far more likely to irritate them.

Random memo-shooting is, in fact, dangerous. Think of all the things people can do with your memos, all the ways memos can be shared with those for whom they weren't intended, all the words that can be lifted out of context to hurt you. No matter what the official line at your company, memos are discoverable.

I have a friend who's struggling with an offhand comment he put in a memo ten years ago, a disparaging remark about a religious group that was made in jest. Some secretary dutifully filed it, and someone who shouldn't have found it did, and now all hell has broken loose over a decade-old private joke.

Every organization has its Keeper of the Eternal Files. When it comes to a potentially vexing memo or letter, you and I would have long forgotten its existence, but not the Keeper, who'll find that sucker the moment it could mean trouble.

On receiving memos: Just as a cigar is sometimes just a cigar (see chapter on same), **a memo is sometimes only a memo.** Still, office memologists pore over them like archaeologists studying shards, examining every word, rereading every line. What are the memologists looking for? For one, the date, which can be tricky. Maybe you date memos to cover your butt; you date it yesterday, or the day your rival should receive it in the interoffice mail. "Gosh, Boss," you say, "I sent her a memo a while ago so she had lots of time . . ." The truth is you sent it yesterday knowing that the mail room is so screwed up that your target wouldn't get it until this morning, which was too late.

The memo's signature can convey meaning. For instance, a memo from the CEO usually implies urgency. But occasionally memos arrive via the CEO that represent someone else's hobbyhorse. These aberrant memos from the CEO can imply a great deal about the pecking order. If the CEO signs an unusual statement, such as a memo on being kind to animals, and the guy across the hall is well-known for his work at the ASPCA, that guy's been designated a protected species.

The signature can also tell you how the company wants you to treat the memo. At times I would sign briefing memos simply to communicate that the memo wasn't as big a deal as it would have been had the CEO signed it, in which case he would have had to include a paragraph saying "Don't take this too seriously"—which would have made everyone take it too seriously.

Memologists also study distribution lists. Standard distribution isn't meaningful, but when the list includes someone surprising, that's almost as interesting as the absence of someone you'd expect.

Tip: **If a memo's truly important, it's probably short.**
Whatever shows up in a memo is generally already office knowledge.
However, memos do serve as confirmation, which can be handy
when you've already put most of the puzzle together.

A wide range of memos courses through offices like blood
through the body. Here are a few:

The Lateral Handoff: This is the least welcome kind. Its purpose
is to shift responsibility from others to you. Basically it says: "Now
that I've reviewed File X, I want you to look at it, too." An in-basket
filled with these can ruin an entire week.

The Serf and Turf: Sometimes a memo from on high is purely
territorial; it tells the plebeians below not to touch something, such as
a new client or a resource. Although it may sound to the unenlight-
ened reader to be nothing more than a statement of fact—"I'm excited
to say that the firm has won the Huge Account, which I will be heading up"—what it means is: Approach at your own risk.

The Cattle Brand: This one is defensive. Let's say that you and I
have talked about an idea, and I know you're an idea rustler, since
you've stolen some of my ideas before. So I send you a thinly veiled
memo to the effect of "I'd like to follow up on our discussion of such-
and-such a project, because after some careful thought, I've decided
that my original idea needs these three steps, and I wonder if you can
help me with them." In other words, it's my idea and now that fact is
on file.

The Boomerang: Remember, where you stand is related to
where you sit. Writing a hot memo calling someone in another department a jerk will not only guarantee that you'll be transferred over
there but that someone in that department will have a copy of the unfortunate memo displayed prominently for all to read.

The Oreo: Let's say your rival Etta has just distributed a memo
about new product pricing. You now send out a memo to the same
distribution list and repeat much of what Etta has already men-

tioned—"Yes, we should increase the price of the New Blah-Blah, and yes, the Blah-Blah is terribly exciting." Then, many paragraphs later, sandwiched between one blah and another, you include a sizzling paragraph that suggests a disturbing weakness in Etta's plans. Then back to blah, blah. The memo looks supportive, so you seem like a team player. But anyone reading the memo carefully—which means barely a soul—knows what you're up to.

The Postmeeting Reality Memo: Companies that are bureaucratic to the point of being arthritic will disseminate memos after a meeting, theoretically to memorialize decisions. Their real purpose is to prevent people from lying about what they said in that meeting. Therefore, whoever drafts these postmeeting memos creates reality, because his version of what happened becomes the official story. History was always thus.

A tale for our times: Hal, a young Silicon Valley techie, when asked about an in-box filled with memos, didn't understand the question. "You mean that stuff that gets sent via snail mail?" At some companies, the written memo has given way entirely to electronic versions, saving thousands of forests but creating thousands of additional interchanges. The rules are still the same. You don't need hard copy to be softheaded.

—⤢ The Evil Twin on memos: The Evil Twin must be very careful here. Leaving behind such recognizable footprints can be dangerous. Furthermore, the print memo's effectiveness has been weakened by the advent of advanced technology; there are so many alternatives to snail mail that memos don't pack the potential for evil they once did.

So the Evil Twin bottom line on memos is to avoid writing them. Instead, let your Evil Twin take advantage of other people's memo mistakes. For example, arch-rival Emily sends you a memo in which she reveals her distaste for your ally Charlotte. Charlotte's not on the distribution list, but that doesn't mean that you can't take one of the

Evil Twin's favorite accessories—the little yellow sticky note—and attach it to the memo with a message to Charlotte: "Perhaps you might be interested in reading this." (The great advantage of that piece of sticky yellow paper is that, unlike a memo, you can scribble whatever you want on it. Those notes aren't made for posterity; they tend to fall off and disappear into the garbage very quickly.)

Or you can even hand the memo to Charlotte yourself and really drive the message home.

Another tactic: Emily writes a memo that you think exposes her vulnerability, her stupidity, or any other frailty. Take that memo to the Big Boss and ask, "Is this really what you want?" You must appear neutral, in control, and puzzled. And it should seem coincidental that you are showing the Big Guy that your rival is proposing something that is completely inconsistent with his position, or otherwise flawed beyond fixing.

Still one more Evil Twin ploy: Emily sends out a dumb memo. This time your goal is to make sure that your co-worker Anne understands just how wrongheaded Emily is. Since your fear is that Anne won't read the long-winded report, you go to her, waving the memo, and ask, with wide-eyed innocence, "Can you translate this for me?"

Now, to explain it, she's forced to read it aloud—and Emily's attempt at wisdom falls flat. Even great memos seldom stand up to oral interpretation.

NOTHING BUT THE TRUTH

There are lies, and then there are lies.

Hank, the president of a consulting outfit, had flown into a large midwestern city where flat plains surround the central urban core. Hank was meeting with a Big Company in one of the city's tallest buildings, but since he was a habitual oversleeper, he was running late. So on his way downtown Hank called Big Company to say that his tardiness was due to a huge traffic jam. Why, he said, Route 555 was so snarled that he'd barely moved a mile since he got into his car.

The only problem was that everyone waiting for him in Big Company's conference room could see Route 555 from the window. There was no traffic jam. Somewhere between amused and angry, the staff turned on the squawk box and the entire room listened to Hank invent a virtual play-by-play of his mythical jam.

Hank knew the meeting didn't go well, but to this day he doesn't know why.

Everyone lies. People who claim that they don't lie are lying. But there's no reason to stop lying completely. Lies are the social lubricant that get us through the day without more confrontation, more anger, more recrimination.

Control your lying, and lie sensibly.

In other words, lie within the culture of fabrications at your company.

This varies widely. A lie at one company may be an aggressive sales tactic at another; a routine rounding-off in one budget report is someone else's concept of cheating. The key is to pay attention to the kinds of lies your company allows, or disavows.

The most common category of lies is the expense account lie. But even though account padding is culturally determined, I personally think it's foolish to lie about expenses. Years ago a co-worker was fired for a $40 lie and it sunk in: I never saw any reason to jeopardize my career over a few bucks.

And I've fired people for lying about company funds. I once had an employee whose overtime claims kept rising until, suspicious, we discovered that many of these overtime hours had taken place on nights while the man was on vacation. But instead of confessing when confronted, the man lied. Bad move. **When they start questioning you about your lies, it means the truth is out.** Toughing it out won't work. It's over. Admit it, grovel in mortification (see chapter on same), promise not to do it again (and genuinely mean it). Then hope for the best.

At some companies, however, you're expected to pad your expense account, particularly in low-paying jobs where they can justify your pitiful salary by paying for your meals. There's still no reason to be sensational. Even when padding is routine, spending $250 on your mother at the best restaurant in town and writing down "Dinner with Hillary Clinton" is wrong. **Don't throw fibs in other people's faces.**

Another kind of lie concerns company resources. Let's say your company forces you to drive often and pays for the gas. What do you do when you go thirty miles out of the way to pick up a special present for your kid? Do you charge the company? Most people do. Is that a lie? Yes. A bad lie? Probably not. A majority of these judgment calls depend on the nature of the company. If your company allows for a little leeway, take it, but no more. Excess padding smells.

Still another major category of lies contains those told in order to avoid saying no. Few people like saying no. They'd rather change the subject, run away, or lie. So many a lie is actually a not-yes: "Do you want to have lunch Monday?" "I'd love to, but I've got to work." Maybe she does, maybe she doesn't. If it's a lie, it wasn't designed to impress you with how much work she has. She said it so that she didn't have to reject you.

These kinds of white lies are necessary. For instance, someone new shows up in your department, and your first impression is negative. Keep it to yourself. "What do you think about Perry?" a friend asks. Don't say, "He's a fool." Say, "I haven't seen enough of him to form an opinion." That's not true, but it's okay. Or if you refuse to lie, obfuscate. Find one nice thing about him—"He sure wears clean clothes."

The bottom line: **It's better to lie about your feelings than about reality.** Lying about numbers will cost you someday, but everyone lies about emotions, and that's okay, particularly when it's to spare someone else's feelings.

The Good Lie: You're at a conference with a colleague who's giving a presentation. He's nervous as hell and it shows. Halfway through his speech, during a coffee break, he asks for your opinion. Don't say, "You stink to high heaven." Say, "Terrific." Your support may give him the confidence to calm down.

The Bad Lie: You and a colleague are working on a report, and you haven't done all your homework. So you fudge your numbers and turn in bad ones to make the deadline. Who do you think you're fooling? Numbers aren't emotions: They can't change because you've lied about them.

The worst place to lie: résumés. Once résumés were taken at face value, but now people check them carefully. You're allowed to embellish your accomplishments, but never say you did something you didn't.

Another bad place to lie: references. For the most part, large companies no longer allow you to discuss former employees, because they're afraid of liability. But if someone asks you informally about a former worker, you have to respond.

If you like the worker, there's no problem. If you don't like the worker, then engage in truth management. Someone asks you about Dana, whom you think is basically incompetent. Find something else to say. "Tell me about the job Dana is applying for," you ask. Let's say your friend wants someone who can do skills A, B, and C. "Dana is excellent at skills X, Y, and Z," you then say. And then you say something nice.

In the long run, lying takes up too much energy. I know one man who lies constantly about everything from his lunch dates (he makes excuses rather than tell people he doesn't want to eat with them) to his contacts (he pretends to know far more important people than he does). How does he keep it all straight? By telling so many people so many different stories, he must spend half his night trying to remember who's been told what. Why does he do it? He wants to be liked. Such people are dangerous. For them words are instruments to be used for currying favor rather than for conveying the truth, which means everything they say has to be taken with a grain of salt. And too much salt causes high blood pressure.

Tip: Most companies have at least one pathological liar in their midst; if that person happens to be your boss, you need a strong defense. Try to hold conversations in front of others, and learn how to write good cover-your-butt memos. As a practice, this isn't a great way to live, but if your boss is that bad, you may not have a choice.

Many more bosses use a certain kind of lie: the nonresponsibility response. They ask you to do something, but the moment you've left the room, any knowledge of that request disappears with you.

Let's say your boss tells you to go and sack Carthage. So you do, and a few weeks later you come back with bloody heads. Meanwhile, your boss has formed an alliance with Carthage.

"What have you done?" he screams. You say, "You told me to." He says, "I did not."

Correct course of action: Send confirming notes without looking too obvious—add other content to disguise your real purpose. For instance, you write, "Boss, you mentioned today you want me to sack Carthage. I'm going to have to change my plans a bit and leave on Sunday instead of Monday. If all goes well, I should come back with fifteen heads." After you've sent a couple of these memos, your boss will figure out what you're up to, and either he'll take more responsibility for his commands or your job will get worse. Either way, you'll have a better sense of whether you can work for him—and for how long.

Tip: One good method of discerning whether people are liars is to take up golf. **People who lie on the golf course lie at the office.** They lift their ball, they take too many mulligans, they change their score. My friend Mallory started playing golf in large part for personnel reasons. Last year she wasn't sure about one man, so she golfed with him. At the seventh hole, he took ten strokes, and then told Mallory he was going to call it an even eight. He lost the game and Mallory's confidence.

Tip: People who can't lie require special handling. My doctor, Rachel, had a receptionist, Phoebe, who believed lying was a sin. Dr. Rachel didn't expect this to be a problem, but she discovered, on Phoebe's first day, that it's impossible to work with an aggressive truth-teller. Phoebe wouldn't cover for Rachel, even though part of her job required screening calls. For instance, when Rachel didn't want to talk to Monica, a cold-calling pharmaceutical salesperson, Phoebe refused to tell Monica that Rachel was out of the office. Instead, Rachel had to walk to the office door and extend a leg toward the hall. "She can't talk to you now," Phoebe then announced. "She's got one foot out the door." Phoebe soon had one foot out the door herself.

⟼ The Evil Twin on lying: Your Evil Twin is in a position to lie only if you've been rigorously truthful for years: You've always taken your share of responsibility when blame is being doled out and you've always been scrupulous with data of all stripes. That's how you build the reputation that you're Someone to Whom Attention Should Be Paid. You're honest. You're decent.

But if you've done all this, then the Evil Twin doesn't have to resort to lying. As noted, lying seldom works. The real trick is being able to point out credibly that others are liars. That makes you the office barometer of who tells the truth and who doesn't. And that makes you a force to be reckoned with.

Not that you would ever actually call someone an out-and-out liar. Crassness is unnecessary. Subtlety is required. Here's the situation: You're angry at Hugh, whose lies have been getting in the way of everyone else's ability to get good work done. Hugh's lies are widespread: It wasn't his fault that his team was late (but it was); he didn't blow the numbers on his budget (but he did). Now Clarissa comes into your office to tell you the latest story about how Hugh wouldn't cop to having botched a project.

You don't call Hugh a liar. All you have to do—you, the well-known truth-teller—is respond, "Sure. And we all know about Hugh. . . ." Then you hold Clarissa's gaze for just a moment longer than necessary. And now you've called Hugh a liar without actually having said so.

SHOW ME THE MONEY

Basically, this whole book is about money. That's why people go to offices. Not that power and prestige aren't important to some (and a few well-adjusted people find enjoyment in actual tasks), but for most, money is the lure.

Asking for money is routinely covered by the press, and dozens of magazines run annual articles with titles along the lines of "How to Ask the Big Boss for the Big Raise, and How to Get It, Too." What they fail to mention, however, is that by the time you do ask for that raise, the Big Boss has already made the decision about whether or not you're going to get it.

The truth is, you have to do everything right before you show up in the boss's office. These decisions don't take place in a vacuum. In business, as in sex, there's a certain point of no return, past which both partners know what's going to happen. We know what we're going to request, they know what they're prepared to give. The general terms have already been established.

The political end of this negotiation involves how to handle the boss's response. For those times when you get what you wanted, there's not much to say: Control your glee; don't name your firstborn after the boss. When you don't get what you want, be practical.

For the most part, bosses say no in several ways.

The most common form of denial is the Maybe Later response. This may or may not be accompanied by an explanation, such as there's a freeze on, or there's no money in this year's budget. What they're really saying is that they don't want to disturb the equilibrium; it would be politically incorrect for you, and only you, to get a raise. Your best response to this? Don't let it drop. Promise secrecy. If they're willing to bend the rules, you won't tell your colleagues. If they still don't budge, ask if you can pick up some extra responsibilities, so that in a few months, when you ask again, you've made yourself look like less of an exception.

Another common rejection is the I Feel Your Pain reply. They're sympathetic, they understand, they care—but they don't budge. Here they're not even holding out the promise of something later or excusing their refusal. So you know: They don't care if you go. So think about going. Empathy is meaningless when it comes to money, but it can be cashed in later for guilt. If these people have the human hearts they claim to have, they'll feel bad when you leave for elsewhere, and they'll become among your most valuable contacts; just don't push their guilt buttons every time you see them.

Then there's the When You Get Bigger ploy, where they come back at you with some kind of senseless condition. "Herman, I understand you want a raise, but I need to see something from you first, and that's more of a presence. I want you to make a bigger impact when you walk into a room. When I see that, I'm confident I can give you a raise."

This kind of response demands that you get an endorsement from some third party whose judgment they value. For instance, if they're saying you don't have enough presence, arrange an opportunity to do something sexy in front of your chosen Mr. Big, who can then rave to your boss about your charisma. However, since this is all so intangible, it may be impossible to prove you have whatever it is they want to see.

The Purely Cosmetic response guarantees you're getting something—a slight raise, an incremental title change—but not as much as you wanted. The good news here is that you're not sticking out, so you're not about to get fired. If that's enough, stay put. But these little bones are like strikes. One cosmetic raise isn't that bad; you can let it slide. Two means you're in trouble. And three is bad—you've been slow-tracked for life.

Then there's the same Don't You Know There Are Starving Children in China gimmick that you got as a child when you didn't finish your dinner. In other words, you should be happy to have a job; plenty of others don't. For the most part there's no good rebuttal here, since it's not a rational argument. So the best approach is to try to make the debate a rational one, which you can do with the Trickle Down theory ("But keeping me productive is good for me, and therefore good for the firm, and therefore good for everyone") or the Reframe, in which you take the argument in a different direction ("I think the real issue here is overstaffing, or population control. What if we discussed ways to eliminate unnecesary staff [and therefore create more money for me]?").

Finally, there's the If You Don't Like It, Ask Your Father response. This, too, is as effective as it was when you were a kid. Your mother already knows your father will say no, since they've agreed to stick together. So when your boss informs you he can't do it but you can try going to his boss, or Human Resources, or headquarters, you're probably sunk. Anyway, it's always dangerous to go directly to Dad to lobby. I've seen people get fired for no less. The problem is you generally have to insult Mom during your plea. And that's never a good idea.

Tip: Don't put your hand out immediately following a success. After you've made a major effort that benefits the company, simply express your appreciation at having been able to help. Wait as long as your patience allows. Only then do you venture, "I want to talk about my future." If you ask for money the moment you've succeeded, not only do you look greedy, it makes them wary of letting you succeed again. **No boss wants to feel like a slot machine.**

Second Tip: Keep your compensation a secret. It's tempting to trust your best friend, but you just don't know what he'll do with the information. "Gee," he says to himself a few hours later, "if little Sandy's making $100,000, and I'm twice as good, I should be making $200,000." Little good can come from this. And what happens when you're no longer friends?

A Final Tip: Money can't buy love. Some of the worst bosses I've ever seen routinely pay 20 percent above market to attract employees. Look before you leap into a new job. If you know that a boss, or a company, is paying too much, find out why. Normally these kinds of salaries are accompanied by revolving doors. Don't be surprised if, a few months after getting that first large paycheck, you're spinning out the door yourself.

—⚭ The Evil Twin on money: A friend of mine figured out how to use her Evil Twin to find out if she was going to be promoted, using money as a yardstick. Sharon was one of the highest-ranking women at her firm, but she knew (one of the secretaries had told her) that every man at her level made more than she did. So she broke one of the essential rules about money, and when it came time to have a discussion with her boss, she purposefully asked for a raise that was far and above a sensible request but that would put her in the same salary category as her male peers. She didn't expect the boss to agree, but she knew that in his answer she'd learn where she stood in the firm's eye. If he held out the promise of reaching a salary level equal to the guys', she'd know she had an equal future, too.

But instead all she got was a speech on how well she was doing and how proud everyone was of her—and no significant raise. Because her boss was smart, he knew what she was really after, and in his way he was letting her know her future at the company—she was liked, she was respected, but she wasn't going any further.

You Are Not Alone

*(Dealing with Other People,
Whether They Like It or Not . . .)*

CONSIDER THE SOURCE

CORPORATE COCKROACHES

A FAVOR THEY CAN'T REFUSE

GOSSIP IS GOOD

HATFIELDS AND McCOYS

THE JOHN WAYNE SYNDROME

OTHER PEOPLE'S POLITICS

SOMETIMES A CIGAR IS JUST A CIGAR

UPSTAIRS, DOWNSTAIRS

WHO'S AFRAID OF VIRGINIA WOOLF?

WITCH DOCTORS

CONSIDER THE SOURCE

A typical scene: You're having lunch with your friend Martin, whom you've always thought was a relatively decent guy. The two of you are on the same career track and were hired at the same time. You're talking about dull, routine stuff until Martin casually lets slip that a senior manager, Conrad, recently commented that you always struck him as a lone wolf. You're startled.

Martin notices your reaction, reconsiders, and backs off. "Oh, you know Conrad," he says. "Always carping."

The conversation moves elsewhere. But that Sunday night your mind keeps returning to Martin's words the way your tongue revisits a sore place on your gum: You know you shouldn't bother it, but it's driving you nuts. You'd been thinking that you were doing pretty well. Why does Conrad believe you're not a team player? Does that mean you're in trouble?

Then it suddenly occurs to you that this is becoming a pattern: Over the last few months Martin's been subtly letting you in on a lot of other people's criticisms. So was Conrad really giving you flak? Or was it actually Martin?

Everyone speaks from his or her own agenda. Each piece of spoken information that finds its way to your ears inevitably has some kind of spin on it, determined by the biases of whoever's speaking. Even if the speaker doesn't consciously intend to spin, he's doing so. He's repeating a long conversation he had with someone else: He can't remember every word he heard, so he edits out the parts he deems unnecessary. That editing itself reflects an agenda.

The way he tells it—how he emphasizes words that are important to
him—is often as significant as the content itself. Facial expressions are
also revealing, as is body language. A shrug. A lifted eyebrow. A roll
of the eyes. Everyone consciously or unconsciously influences how
the other person receives their words.

Some of the time we're sensitive to these signals, such as when
we're talking to an enemy and all our antennae are extended. Other
times we forget about personal agendas, particularly when we get so
caught up in a piece of gossip that we forget to look for the spin.

And sometimes that spin is so slight you may think it doesn't
matter. But watch out: The same small spin repeatedly coming from
the same person can be meaningful.

Years ago I had an employee named Arch who was smart and
fun, and who gave me valuable feedback on other people's opinions.
"Gloria doesn't like you," he'd say. Feeling hurt, I'd then share my
opinion of Gloria with him. And when hurt, I seldom had positive
things to say. But Arch never failed to tell me whenever he heard
something negative about me. "Rob thinks you screwed up," he'd
say. "Edith's concerned you don't have the right background for this
job."

One day, years into Arch's comments, a lightbulb finally went off
in my head. Arch was about to pass along another insult when I suddenly realized that it was only Arch who brought these criticisms to
my attention. My own experience never uncovered such a large cache
of ill will, and other employees, who shared greater confidences with
me, didn't have such unfailingly bad news.

What was Arch up to? Making himself feel better, I decided.
Over the years he had built up a good deal of resentment about how
fast my career had progressed, but he couldn't tell me this directly;
he didn't know how to communicate his own negative feelings. Instead, his repressed anger reappeared in the form of these comments.

The next time Arch started to tell me that someone thought I'd
made a terrible mistake, I interrupted to say how much I cared for

that person. He changed the topic. When he tried again, I shut him off again. Eventually Arch stopped, but not before I must have expressed affection for dozens of people who didn't really matter to me one way or another.

Misinformation happens. People are always trying to line you up on their side, or to get you to go after their enemy, or to have you do them a favor. And they usually believe they'll have a better chance of getting what they want by asking for it in a disguised manner. Therefore, much of what they pass along tends to be heavily weighted toward their own needs, and not yours.

Is there a quick and easy way to determine what people really mean and what's really true? No. You can't know; at least, not in the short term. You just have to train yourself to weigh all the options. Consider why you may be hearing what you're hearing. Judge it in many contexts. Ask yourself, "What are some other reasons why I'm getting this message?" The possibilities may amaze you.

Note: Some people are magnets for other people's agendas. For example, folks who work closely with the Big Boss hear nothing but pleasantly packaged rubbish day and night, because everyone thinks it's a way to curry favor. "Maybe she'll pass along something good about me," the speaker thinks, complimenting Ms. Assistant on her new hairstyle, not realizing that he's one of a hundred who've done the same that day.

⚡ The Evil Twin on misrepresentation: The Evil Twin has a big mouth. For instance, someone shows you a project he's been developing. You look at it, you judge it, but then your Evil Twin jumps in to tell you how to spin your response. If you're talking to an enemy, do you point out its flaws and try to weaken his resolve? Or if it's truly bad, do you tell him it's good so he'll share it with others? Or perhaps you tell him that it has some problems but you can help him, because at some level you know that he's onto something big and you'd like a piece of it.

The Evil Twin often makes an appearance when it's time to pass along information. Most of the time you should ignore your twin's thoughts.

When the situation involves someone else's Evil Twin interpreting reality for you, throw it back in his face. For instance, I could have said to Arch, "I wonder why Gloria would tell you these things," implying that there was something I knew about the two of them that he didn't. In other words: Make the other person consider the source, too. The messenger will then obsess about his own potential problems, not yours.

CORPORATE COCKROACHES

Most corporations have their share of company insects, whether it's the gadflies in the boardroom or the slugs in the basement. Corporate cockroaches, however, are universal. Like their namesakes, they're survivors; they've been there since the company was born, and they'll be there after the company's gone—they'll survive a neutron bomb, show up at the office the next morning, and ask, "Where is everybody?" They're the bureaucrats who never change, the functionaries who are impervious to all corporate machinations.

They also get all the tasks done, by the way. While everyone else is posturing and maneuvering, these are the solid people who finish the contracts, assign the paperwork, record the files. They know everything, and they're beyond caring. They're not good or bad. They're not mean or nice. They just are.

As with their insect cousins, if you see one or two of them, there's a strong possibility others are around, hidden behind the walls. The organization that grows one or two grows many.

Cockroaches hang out together, they lunch together, they have drinks together. Their only issue is survival, and their primary goal in life is to fight change. So if you're toeing the line, you can tiptoe around them without a problem.

But if you're trying to implement change, then you're going to have to deal with them. **If corporate cockroaches get in your way, step on them quickly.** Otherwise they'll swarm after you in ways you never thought possible, attacking through walls and floors and making appearances where you thought no corporate being could exist. They know the corporation better than you do. They know all its ups and downs and exits and entrances. If you don't deal with them quickly, they'll carry you out later.

Plenty of other insects infest the corporate structure. There are the ticks, who need your blood to survive. When you show up at an office, all bright-eyed energy and stamina—those ticks can smell that fresh blood of yours. They'll have some agenda to pursue, and since they don't have their own energy source, they'll try to get at yours to fuel their drive. They'll make their approach, oozing complaints: This project's a failure, So-and-So is a jerk, these problems are disastrous. What they're really saying is "Fix it for me." Listen to ticks; they'll tell you where the bloody messes are. But don't declare any allegiances or get too close. You don't want to walk around with bloodstains on your legs.

Then there are the corporate butterflies, who flit around the power source. They have no power of their own, but their physical beauty or inherent charm allows them the kind of access to the Big Boss that everyone else covets. They fulfill no real purpose, but the Big Boss allows them to survive because they're too decorative to destroy.

If your company is large, you've already seen the worker ants. They inhabit most of the floors between the lobby and the power floors, and they do a significant share of the work. They no longer expect to advance, but unlike the roaches, their allegiance isn't to the site but to the work itself. If the hill is disrupted, they'll go off in search of another.

—⚔ The Evil Twin on corporate insects: It's a far, far more evil thing than I would ever do, but if faced with a loathsome enemy, the Evil Twin can mobilize the wrath of the cockroaches by indicating to them that your enemy is an agent of change. This will cause great aggravation in the nest, and while your enemy may be on guard, awaiting evil things from you, he won't be expecting a flying squadron of brown bugs that can take him down faster and more effectively than you ever could.

Such a scenario unfailingly unfolds when, much to the discontent of the insiders, an outsider is brought in to run a company. Outsiders are usually given a mandate to make changes, and as was mentioned earlier, change doesn't sit well with corporate arthropods.

I recently observed this phenomenon when a friend was asked to take over a large health-related concern.

Trevor was a shrewd cost-cutter and an agile thinker, but he was one of those people who thought he was smarter than everyone else. Maybe he was, but he wasn't smart enough to realize that being smart isn't enough.

Trevor had been brought in over the heads of three senior vice presidents, none of whom were happy about the situation. Two of these men reacted passively and sat back, ready to collect their paychecks as ever. The third man, Orson, was livid, and decided to defend his turf. His plan? Orson enlisted the aid of the cockroaches, who, in a company where the constant flow of money was the lifeblood of the organization, were capable of impeding that flow.

Orson enlisted this aid by placing the fear of God in those cockroaches. He initiated a series of statements that implied huge changes under Trevor's regime. Orson talked about systems upgrades (which created fear of wide-scale dismissals), reorganization (which created fear of painful restructuring), and cost cutting (which frightened everyone else, too).

It worked. Systems became clogged. Routine tasks weren't being finished. The bottom line nose-dived. Trevor wasn't fired, but Orson ended up being promoted to an equal partner, and as of this moment, they're still fighting. But the cockroaches have made it clear where their sympathies lie, and I wouldn't bet against them.

A FAVOR THEY CAN'T REFUSE

Do you remember how *The Godfather*'s Don Corleone was always doing small things for others long before they did anything for him? And when the recipients of such unexpected largesse asked what they could do in return, he always told them that the time for gratitude would come.

Follow this model. **Do as much as you can for the right people before being asked.**

Who are the right people? People in whom you believe, people on your wavelength who you feel are capable of understanding the rules of giving and taking—the people your gut tells you you'd like to have on your team.

The more connected you are to such people, the easier it is to get work done. You'll all want to achieve similar results, and you'll seek out ways to help each other.

Most important: Always go out of your way to do nice things for those who are in trouble.

People don't forget that you were there when they needed help. When the time comes, they'll be there for you, too. Don't you remember everyone who helped when you were suffering?

But if you're out of work, and no one's calling to help, it's because you were never there for anyone else. You were too busy for a lunch, you couldn't talk to that co-worker's nephew who just graduated from college, you didn't buy a raffle ticket for the Little Sisters of the Poor bazaar. Now that you have nothing to offer, no one's going to return your calls.

—✦ The Evil Twin on favors: Watch for that rare moment when dol-
ing out a swanky favor to rack up points is indeed the right move.
Perhaps there's someone in the organization from whom you need
something. You wait for the right moment, and then you pounce.

Here's an example from Carole, whose boss was notably difficult
and ornery: A few summers ago her company sent her and the boss
to a one-month training program, during the course of which the
boss underwent a midlife crisis with the speed of time-lapse photog-
raphy, engaging in more sexual encounters in four weeks than he'd
had in the previous ten years.

At the program's end, the boss's wife showed up and remarked
to Carole that she could tell how much her husband had missed her
because he seemed so completely exhausted (he was—he'd barely had
any time to sleep). Carole solemnly agreed that the husband had, indeed, been pining away for Mrs. Boss. Then she confided in her
boss's best friend, letting him know what she'd done, knowing full
well that he'd tell the Big Guy. Now both she and the boss knew that
the next time she needed something . . .

GOSSIP IS GOOD

Every company maintains some official form of communication that appears regularly on people's desks or computer screens and pronounces, "This is reality."

No one who's smart believes it.

An office memo, or any other centrally generated communication, is meaningless until you uncover its true significance.

For instance, a memo comes across your desk saying that a Mr. Forrest Gump has been named executive director of the new Organization Department. You don't have a clue what this fancy title means. Was the man kicked upstairs? Was he demoted? You're not even sure what the new Organization Department is. Gossip is the only way to fill in blanks left by office propaganda.

Everyone says that gossip is a bad thing. Not true. It's the octane on which organizations run. It's also very efficient, because it's targeted. Only those people who really want to know, and are meant to know, are included. And gossip spreads quickly and is always brief and interesting—there's no such thing as three pages of dull gossip.

Gossip is bad only when it's meant to be personally destructive. Still, sometimes even that type of information can be useful—as long as you don't pass it along. For instance, a secretary once told me about a senior vice president's drinking problem, which occasionally led to unwanted passes. A few months later, when this VP offered me a ride home in his limo after an office party, I knew enough to check whether he was asking me or if the martinis were. One glance told me it was the latter. Gossip had given me the information I needed to make the right call.

Gossip guideline: **Never violate a confidence.** Don't pass anything along until you've heard it from at least three people. Otherwise, you run the risk of exposing your sources, in which case you'll never hear anything from them again. And once you're out of the loop, you won't have access to the inside story.

The Evil Twin on gossip: My friend Morris once came to me seeking advice about a loathed co-worker named Catherine. Morris and Catherine were on the same track for promotion at their office, but whereas Morris tried hard to team with Catherine, believing that a coordinated effort would have been best for both of them, Catherine undercut her rival whenever possible. And when Morris took a one-month paternity leave, Catherine, always affecting the saddest expression in her repertoire, never failed to point out to the Boss how difficult it was for everyone while Morris was away. Then she'd ask, so sincerely, did the Boss really think Morris would be able to concentrate on all the work when (and if) he returned?

But as it turned out, the Boss didn't think any more of Catherine than Morris did, and she began to drop hints to Morris that he, rather than Catherine, was going to be promoted. Not only that, the Boss added, but if Catherine were smart, she might consider updating her résumé.

My advice to Morris: Now that he had a piece of gossip to use, if he was going to use it, he should do so wisely.

Catherine's team consisted of five people, two of whom Morris coveted for his own team. So his first move was to hint to these two people that Catherine was in trouble. He never came out and said it, for that would have sent them running to Catherine for verification, which in turn would only have created havoc. Instead, Morris let them know that changes were in the air and that pinning their tails too firmly to the Catherine donkey was a big mistake.

The two workers didn't let Morris down. They proved their intelligence by scoping out the truth, and were sufficiently able to distance themselves from Catherine before she was fired. For that, they owed an eternal debt of gratitude to Morris, who soon had them working overtime.

The moral for the Evil Twin: Never serve gossip raw. Process it intelligently, dole it out selectively, reap the rewards discreetly.

HATFIELDS AND McCOYS

Everywhere, in every office all over the world, each person plays a given role, and often these roles are in natural conflict with one another. Just as the lion and the jackal are enemies on the savannah, the people who oversee the money and the people who run the sales department are always going to fight. The guys on the planning staff are usually at war with the people who run businesses. The woman in charge of the northern territories is battling with the guys in charge of the western, eastern, and southern territories. Same story with manufacturing and marketing. Creatives and suits. How do you think the term *suits* was invented, if not by irritated creatives?

But just as nature has a master plan, so does business. Intramural feuding is essential to the natural selection process. **Feuding is good for business survival.**

An organization shouldn't be cozy. Absolute comfort creates languor, which invites predators. Imagine if every time you exceeded your budget, the CFO said, "Hey, who cares? It's only an extra million." Or if a creative said to a suit, in the middle of a new business pitch, "I've just realized that breakthrough ideas aren't important. Our real goal should be holding down overtime costs."

Territorial fights are to be encouraged, with artisans fighting for their guilds. If there's no sparring, your company's headed for trouble. Even more important than the fighting, though, is how the battles are perceived by the warriors.

Let's say your job running a large operation requires that you make on-the-spot decisions all day and most of the night. Someone comes to you with an emergency and needs $10,000 pronto. So you find the money on a different budget line and liberate it for this unanticipated expense.

Now let's say that Rhoda's in charge of your budget, and the moment she sees those numbers appear on her screen, she rushes over to you and says, "Listen, you don't have a ten-thousand-dollar slush fund. You can't move funds around on a whim. You've screwed everything up. I'm going to have to go to the Big Boss."

She's unhappy, you're unhappy, and you're especially unhappy with her. And she's not too pleased with you, either.

Fights like this happen all the time. It's easier if you expect them and are emotionally prepared. Not that you shouldn't become angry. But you have a choice as to whether you manage the situation or let your anger manage it.

Here's the trick: Don't personalize these feuds. You'll want to. Before Rhoda's out the door, you'll be thinking, "That miserable little bean counter is out to get me. I'll show her." But even though it's hard to believe at this moment, Rhoda actually isn't out to get you. She probably doesn't even care about you. It's all about your role. If you transferred over to Accounting tomorrow, you and Rhoda could very well become best buddies, plotting against your current comrades.

So if you're regularly having these kinds of fights, it probably means you're just doing your job, and you can relax. There are plenty of ways to avoid the hurt feelings that accompany squabbles. Find outlets through which you can vent your emotions in harmless arenas. Organize company-wide projects to air out some of that aggression and tension.

For instance: I know one place that sponsors an annual lawyers vs. rest-of-staff softball game. As in most places, the lawyers are roundly despised, and the game allows everyone to say what they aren't supposed to say but want to. It's not cool to go into Lawyer

Jones's office and say, "Nyah, nyah, you can't read, you can't write." But on the softball field you can yell, "Nyah, nyah, you can't hit, you can't run." (Lawyers being lawyers, last year they hired a former college all-star pitcher as a paralegal, put him on the mound, and won 12–0.)

—⚓ The Evil Twin on feuds: The following strategy is one that you should use only if you're sincerely convinced that the person you're going after is truly malevolent. In that rare case, play off his natural insecurity. (As a rule, however, territorial office feuds should never become personal, since that's where the hurt starts, and hurt feelings lead to grudge matches, which lead to death fights, which lead to blood on the floor, which leads to everyone sliding around instead of working.)

So the Evil Twin makes a necessary exception by personalizing the impersonal. Let's go back to Rhoda, the bean counter who snarls at anyone who gets in the way of her numbers. As a result, she treats everyone in exactly the same unpleasant manner, including Joe, your despised rival. Fool with Joe's insecurities. After Rhoda's gone on the warpath, carrying on about everyone's budgets, amble down to Joe's office. "Hey," you offer, "isn't it amazing how Rhoda's changed?" Joe looks startled. "Huh?" he says.

"She was so nice to me about my numbers," you continue. "She even suggested places where I didn't have to make cuts. Didn't she do that for you?"

Joe will probably agree with you, but behind those nods lies panic. Does Rhoda really hate him? Why is she picking on him? The truth is that Rhoda was just as difficult with you as always. But Joe doesn't need to know that.

THE JOHN WAYNE SYNDROME

Here comes ol' saddle-weary John Wayne, riding down a dusty Main Street in some godforsaken community, when, all of a sudden and from out of nowhere, in runs the local schoolteacher in her plain brown dress and bonnet.

"Help me, help me," she cries. "They're burning down the schoolhouse, they've shot my pa, and now they're torturing my doggie."

John Wayne stares right into the schoolmarm's eye. "Don't worry 'bout a thing, missy," he says. "I'll take care of it." And off he rides to battle the forces of evil. Two hours later, the school is rebuilt, Rover's wagging his tail, and it turns out Pa wasn't dead after all. John Wayne tips his hat and rides off into the sunset.

It's a great scenario, but here's something to consider: You're not John Wayne. Even John Wayne wasn't John Wayne—he was Marion Morrison.

Sad but true: No good deed goes unpunished. Because it upsets their sense of justice, people often protest when they hear this. But it wouldn't be a cliché if so many people didn't say it, and people wouldn't say it so often if it weren't true.

It's no different at the office. One of the major reasons good people land in trouble is that they get suckered into someone else's fight. It always seems like a good idea at the time. There's the suffering schoolmarm, and here you are with your six-shooter. The problem is, in real life you don't know if the schoolmarm's telling you the truth. For all you know, she's the bad guy's dance-hall girlfriend. You don't even know if you have bullets in your gun.

I used to do the John Wayne thing all the time. The instinct to lend a helping hand clicked in, and I'd respond to every seemingly innocent cry for help. My vanity couldn't resist an appeal based on my strength and importance.

Unlike John Wayne, however, I didn't win every time, or even most of the time. Worse, sometimes it turned out that I wasn't even fighting the bad guys. I'd look up midbattle and realize that the guys I thought were bad guys had a good point. Or that the person I was defending had disappeared from the scene. Or that he was the real bad guy in disguise.

Work isn't as simple as the movies. In real life you receive all kinds of information, some of it accurate, some not so accurate, particularly when someone's recruiting you for her team. You also get lots of different outcomes other than victory: You can get slugged, you can become so exhausted you're too tired to fight your own fights, or you can end up slugging someone you think is a bad guy but who turns out to be a good guy.

Now, there certainly are times when you should come to the aid of others. The rule is: **Think before you help.** Help people when it's clear that they're being bullied and you have the ability to do something about it. Help people you have a realistic chance of saving. Help those you respect. Help those who would help you in the same situation, or people who've fought for you before. And step in if it's a battle that you would fight anyway. Otherwise, leave the ring.

—⟨ The Evil Twin on fighting other people's fights: Just as mentioned in Don't Swing at Every Pitch, the trick is simply to ease your enemy into the fray. You and Luis don't get along. Luis suffers from John Wayne–itis. Send supplicants to him, promising them, "I just can't help you on that one, but I know that Luis can."

But be careful: Are you sure Luis deserves to be your enemy? For the most part, people who are willing to fight for others are usually pretty decent folk. Are you setting Luis up because he deserves it or because it would just feel good to have a small triumph?

OTHER PEOPLE'S POLITICS

This is the story of how Emma blew it.

Emma, ten years older than I, was similar to me in many ways, so I liked watching her climb the rungs I hoped lay ahead of me. She was an excellent role model: quick on her feet, smart, charming, accomplished.

After advancing far up the corporate ladder, Emma decided to go off and become a management consultant. Today she's still a role model, but a model of what *not* to do.

One of Emma's prime contacts was Frank, a Mexican-American who'd faced many obstacles on his own strenuous climb to CEO. Frank and Emma had worked well together in the past, so when she went out on her own, Frank was on Emma's short list of prospects.

Frank took Emma's call, which he normally wouldn't have done for just anyone. But since his brand of management was team oriented, Frank arranged for Emma to meet a group vice president, George, who thought Emma had enough good ideas for her to meet his number two, Harriet. That's the way Frank's company worked.

Emma erupted. It was bad enough that Frank sent her to George, but to be passed along to George's Harriet? No way. She stewed, complained, and avoided scheduling time with Harriet, and in doing so, she irritated both George and Harriet, who complained to Frank, ensuring that Emma never got retained.

If Emma had only focused on reality, she'd have taken Harriet to lunch, made a new friend, and landed a big account. Instead, she didn't bother to learn the mechanics of Frank's shop. End of story.

It's tough enough to grasp your own company's politics, but if you're selling something, whether you're in public relations, accounting, advertising, consulting, law, manufacturing, or any of the many industries that perform tasks for other businesses, you're faced with a double whammy: You have to master the politics of their company's politics, too.

Other people's politics can be even more frustrating to understand than your own, since they march to their own rhythm and operate by their own logic—or lack thereof.

One man who works at a software company recently discovered that his outfit and the Enormous Computer Company were competing to sell a software program to one of the big accounting firms. My friend, a logical type, didn't foresee much of a fight since his company had the software ready to go and Enormous didn't. Furthermore, my friend's company was selling its program for 5 percent less than Enormous would sell theirs—once they developed it.

The accounting firm chose Enormous. Why? The decision was made for reasons having little to do with the purchase and everything to do with the existing relationship between Enormous's big cheeses and the accounting firm. My friend discovered that technical merit can get you into the game but it doesn't mean you'll win. Winning takes knowing who keeps score and how they keep it.

There are several things to learn about any company you do business with (or want to):

One: Act as an intelligence agent. Uncover as much as possible about the people who work there. Once you could develop relationships with prospects and clients over time. Once, if I was your lawyer, and I knew you were passionate about the opera, I'd manage to come up with a few great tickets. The point wasn't the money but the precision: giving you exactly what you wanted. Slowly you'd believe I liked you and understood you, which is the key to a truly good client relationship.

Who has that kind of time today? The woman who's acted as your contact for the last five years has left the firm, as has her replacement. So you have to figure out as much as you can as fast as you can. The wrong move is lethal.

Two: Identify the decision makers and those who influence them. Liana ran the advertising end of a packaged goods company, where she farmed out $10 million worth of work to a local ad agency, Louder and Larger. The people at Louder and Larger loved Liana—why shouldn't they, considering how much she was worth to them in commissions? Louder and Larger never bothered to get close to anyone but Liana. So the inevitable day came when Liana's boss hired someone above Liana and she quit in a huff. Suddenly Louder and Larger was scrambling to make other contacts in the organization, but it was too late, and within six months they were gone. Belatedly, Louder and Larger realized that while Liana called the shots on execution, the decisions about what to spend came from a guy two floors up whom they'd never bothered to cultivate.

Three: Find out if you're attached to a loser. I knew a woman who was consulting for a company where the CFO was trying to bump off the CEO; therefore, as part of his complicated plan, the CFO fed my friend inaccurate information. She knew something was wrong, but it didn't all come together until she finally realized the CFO was avoiding three-way conversations with her and the CEO. Sure enough, within half a year the CEO was ousted—as was my friend, shortly thereafter.

What do you do in situations like that? Find out as much as possible by meeting everyone in the company you can sensibly meet. Ask them questions and resist your own impulse to talk. Leave long, quiet spaces in the conversation for them to fill, and they will.

Four: You also need to determine if you're attached to people who are terrible at politics, in which case you'll need to know their politics better than they do and coach them without making it obvious that you're doing so.

Five: Dance with your date. Even if the person who retained you is in trouble, and you see a chance to switch alliances, restrain yourself if it means working against the contact who brought you in. Yes, you should know if you're on the losing team, but that's why you align yourself broadly—so when a cord is cut, there's a net underneath. Don't be disloyal (unless sticking around would represent a serious ethical problem). But you can shift into neutral, which means just that: Don't publicly involve yourself either way.

—❦ The Evil Twin on other people's politics: There's no room for argument here—keep your Twin out of it. The relationships your company has forged with others are company resources, like money or talent. They don't belong to you. If you fool around with these, you'll be perceived as someone who would fool around with anything, and it won't take long for people to figure out that if that's the case you're more trouble than you're worth.

SOMETIMES A CIGAR
IS JUST A CIGAR

Lurking somewhere in almost every office is Mr. Hidden Meaning.
You know the guy, the one who's always interpreting what things
"really mean."

"Look at that memo," he says. "Fire regulations? Ha! It's about
who's in power. You see . . ." He settles in for a long explanation.
"People who are made floor fire wardens couldn't have much power,
so what the Big Guy's trying to say is that Mona's no longer at the
same level as me, since I was fire warden two years ago . . ." And he
goes on. And on. Mr. Meaning sees importance in everything,
whether it's a new office policy about using paper cups instead of
mugs at the coffee cart ("The office manager's getting promoted") or
a good-bye card for a retiring employee ("Wake up and smell the
card. He was forced out").

Unless you're a psychiatrist, there's such a thing as overanalysis.
Some things are exactly as they appear. Although we might want to
think we're connected to every action in the world, **people behave
for reasons entirely their own, reasons that have nothing to do with us.** Most people are acting only on their own im-
pulses, in their own world, and no one can penetrate what's really
happening—not even you.

Here's a story from a friend: Arthur was thinking of going into
business with Roger, whom he'd known for years. Roger then announced that he wanted to bring into the enterprise a third partner,
a research analyst named Hester whom Arthur didn't know. At

Roger's suggestion, Arthur called Hester to set up an introductory lunch date. But Hester didn't return Arthur's first call. Or his second. Or his third. Arthur began to melt down. Didn't Hester like what she'd heard about him? Was she having second thoughts about the venture? Was she suggesting somehow that Roger reconsider Arthur as a potential partner?

It never occurred to Arthur that Hester was temporarily overwhelmed by her schedule. Eventually they did make a lunch date, and Arthur was charmed. A cigar was a cigar.

We're most likely to overanalyze when we want something from someone else and that someone else isn't responding. Waiting for the phone to ring when you're hoping for a new job, or a new client, or a plum assignment: It's like waiting for important news from the doctor—it seems to take forever. You're on hold and so is your life. At these times, we ascribe too much importance to the other person's every move—the raised eyebrow, the slight hesitation, the throat clearing.

What we forget is that we're seldom at the top of anyone else's agenda. Just because you're focused on the Big Boss doesn't mean the Big Boss is focused on you. When you walk past her in the hallway and she doesn't say hello, that doesn't mean she doesn't like you, or that you're not getting that bonus. Maybe she's preoccupied with family problems. Maybe she's in a serious hurry to get to the bathroom. She lives in her world; you live in yours.

It's like romance. When you're first in love, everything your lover does has meaning. But how often is your boss in love with you? (If you had to think about that one, reread Zipper Problems.)

A single action can be interpreted in many different ways. Take breaking a lunch date: The first time it happens, it's no big deal; there's no particular meaning. Or is there? The best way to find out is to schedule another one. If that one's broken, that may not signify anything, either, but now there's room for speculation. And if three dates are broken in a row? There's meaning all right. But what? It could be a brush-off. Or maybe the guy in question is one of those people who's so caught up in his own affairs that he can't get unstuck for lunch. But since he wants to be liked, he always consents—and cancels, usually at the last minute.

And then there are those times when someone puts a hand on your shoulder and leaves it there a beat too long. What does that mean? Is it sexy? It is meant to be?

Just as with lunch, you may never know. But if it's part of a larger pattern, you'll eventually figure it out. People reveal themselves over time. What looks like a meaningful moment may simply be an insignificant impulse, best forgotten. But if you see that moment repeated, it's not a moment, it's a message.

—⟨ The Evil Twin on overanalysis: Use it when you want to undermine your enemy's confidence. "So you got invited to the Big Guy's house for dinner," you say to your enemy. "Terrific. Of course, you know what that's about." Smile knowingly. Then leave. Or wait for the one memo where his name was accidentally dropped off and pretend to sympathize with him until your seemingly kind behavior has convinced him he's in trouble.

Or put your office's Mr. Hidden Meaning on the case, and if you catch your enemy in the right paranoid mood, you can destroy his week—or more, particularly if he's not familiar with Mr. Meaning's proclivity for endless analysis.

UPSTAIRS, DOWNSTAIRS

Remember the 1970s British television program *Upstairs, Downstairs*? A similar arrangement occurs in offices. And as in households, subordinates, although they may seem invisible, always wield their own kind of power—and a lot of it. These folks know everything about everyone, which means that they can, and do, shape how the game is played.

For instance: Years ago it was fashionable for secretaries to attach themselves to young comers and hang on for the whole career ride. One re-insurance industry Big Boss I knew kept the same secretary for forty-five years: Miss Primrose. She didn't have a big title or make the big bucks, but she wielded big power.

One day an actuarial vice president named Cheryl walked into the big shot's outer sanctum, looked around, and saw only Miss Primrose. "I guess no one's here," she said, and left the room.

Mysteriously, after that moment, Cheryl's career went into a slump. Mr. Big and his boys had always admired Cheryl's mathematical genius, but now concerns about her managerial style arose—Cheryl's staff didn't like her, Cheryl didn't know how to deal with tension, Cheryl's team was always demoralized. All of this was fed to the boss in subtle yet powerful ways by Miss Primrose, who told me the story herself—rather proudly, in fact.

The moral: **Treat subordinates right and they'll treat you right.**

If you're friendly with people on the lower end of the power spectrum, they'll also let you know early on about other employees'

faults. You'll get a heads-up about who has bad moods, bad mornings, or bad manners. You'll know how they behave when they think
nobody's looking. You'll discover who's sleeping with whom after
hours, and who's asleep during hours. You'll find out more than your
peer gossip could have told you.

The Inverse Rule: **Watch out for peers who treat subordinates badly.** People reveal their character by how they handle the least powerful. If they treat them badly, someday they'll treat
you badly, too.

Caution: If you're new to an office, you can tell if an assistant is
well liked if the company keeps her around after her boss goes down.
You might want to make a play for her, too. But if the boss leaves and
no one else wants her, dig deep before you even consider her for your
team.

Tip: Commiserate. Confide in subordinates that you can't stand
the fluorescent lighting in the offices, or that there's no place to get a
decent cup of coffee nearby. It's an outstanding way to make friends,
particularly among your assistants, because it proves that you're
human and that you suffer as much as they do. Just make sure you
listen in return when they complain, too.

Special situation: sharing a secretary. Here's a story from a
Texas search firm, where two senior people—Nicole and Dick—had
been told, due to cutbacks, that they had to share an assistant, Rosemary. Both Nicole and Dick were already overworked and both felt
that they each needed two assistants, not half of one.

Rosemary was no fool. She knew how her bosses felt and she
played it like the precocious child of divorced parents. Dick, needing
Rosemary to stay late to type a report, attempted to bribe her with a
promise of a bonus. Rosemary made sure Nicole heard about it, and
the next day Nicole came in with her own offer. Dick managed to
hear about this, too, and soon Rosemary got a raise *and* a bonus.
Meanwhile, Rosemary was actually working half-time, since she

knew Dick and Nicole were too angry with each other to confer, so she could always tell one that the other was taking up all her time.

Sharing an assistant can be highly politicized. It's not unlike having joint custody of a child. The rules are similar: Don't use the assistant to deliver messages. Just as you shouldn't say to a child, "Your father's late with the alimony check again," don't force the assistant to pick sides. If you've got a problem, negotiate with the other boss directly. Don't ask the assistant to do the prioritizing.

And when unusual situations arise, give everyone involved as much advance warning as possible: "I want to let you know that I've got a big project coming up next week and I'll need more of little Rosie's time than usual. I'll step back next month when you've got the management committee presentation."

If the other person refuses to be a good parent, be firm and raise the possibility of involving other people in the resolution. Sometimes only a threat is needed to get the other person to behave, not unlike a court order. "We're sharing little Rosie, and my work isn't getting done. And I know you need more time, but so do I. Do you want me to go to the Big Boss and tell him we can't work this out?" Neither of you wants that.

More on subordinates: Q: What's the first thing you should say to a subordinate who brings you bad news? A: Thank you. And then you add a few words about how scary it can be to pass along negative information and that you're very grateful to hear about it. **Coddle the messenger.** Otherwise people will be afraid to tell you things you need to hear.

⚡ The Evil Twin on support staff: You can glean enormous amounts of information from them.

Flora shared an assistant with Miles, her organizational peer—or, in real English, her rival. Miles treated Peter, the assistant, exactly the same way he treated everyone else who wasn't his boss: conde-

scendingly at his best, bullyingly at his worst. Flora also kept to her
basic style: good-natured, low-key, respectful. It didn't take long before Peter figured out who was Gallant and who was Goofus, and au-
tomatically starting helping Flora. As a result, Flora might as well
have had a secret microphone planted on Miles. She knew Miles's
every move, as well as everything Miles said about her. Miles could
never figure it out because he thought that if he and Peter were the
only people present in a room, he was alone.

WHO'S AFRAID
OF VIRGINIA WOOLF?

It's a common Big Screen scenario: Hero has a bad day at the office and brings it home. Sometimes it makes for a classic movie, such as *It's a Wonderful Life*. Sometimes it makes for a violent movie, like *The Untouchables*. Movies aside, it seldom makes for much fun: Spouse returns home, Spouse yells at Spouse, Spouses get angry, Spouses fight, Spouses make up (or they don't). It's not much of a plot, but it's the longest-running show in many households.

There are variants, however. Some spouses are very supportive, some aren't. There is one truism that applies in each and every case: Be wary of your spouse's advice on office tactics. **Just because Spouse pops up the hood doesn't mean Spouse can fix the engine.**

As much as you love your partner—or as much as you don't—your spouse doesn't work with you. Your spouse has a limited view of what's actually happening. Your spouse can only guess what other people are really like, even if your spouse has met them at social events—you can't tell what it's like to work with someone unless you do it.

The other problem is that your spouse doesn't know what you're like to work with, either. You can be the world's most wonderful, caring household partner, but you can still be a bastard to work with, or vice versa. Spouse doesn't know either way.

Here are some of the normal spousal responses to, "Honey, I had a terrible day at the office":

"They're horrible people, all of them."

"You deserve much better than that."

"They don't appreciate how good you are."

"They take you for granted."

This last one packs a double whammy, as it implies you've ignored obvious opportunities to take action. In other words, you should demand a raise, or tell them to go jump in a lake, or kick someone's butt—none of which are appropriate responses.

For the most part, spouses often advocate taking action, since listening seems overly passive. And usually that recommended action is destructive. One of the worst examples I can think of comes from my own marriage.

My husband, Jim, was working at a public relations firm at a time when a new CEO came into the company. Jim had just survived a horrific power struggle but was trailing blood behind him. The new CEO gave him no clue as to whether he was liked or disliked. Jim felt underappreciated. His career was idling.

Meanwhile, we were in the throes of financial chaos, paying both alimony and child support, plus taking care of two kids who were approaching college age.

So I came up with a brilliant idea. The CEO wasn't taking Jim seriously, so why shouldn't Jim write down on paper his clear and clever vision for the firm's future? This could leverage Jim into a position of real power—once the new CEO understood just how bright Jim was.

Jim's reservations were overcome by my enthusiasm, and he went ahead with the plan. But his paper was met with a deafening silence. Things went downhill from there. The CEO hated the document. He thought it was critical of him. Worse, because Jim was working with his own vision, not the CEO's, Jim wasn't perceived as a team player. The strategy couldn't have been more wrong. Jim was justifiably furious at me.

I may be good at my own politics, but I can't coach the person I love most. Which isn't to say that there aren't ways in which spouses can help. For one thing, Jim can translate guy talk for me, and I can decipher gal-speak for him. He can absorb some of my anger and unhappiness, and offer a supportive environment when I bring my troubles home. But few spouses can become the other's career adviser (unless the spouses work together, which is a whole other thorny issue).

I run into bad spousal office politics all the time. One of my closest friends was in deep trouble, but his wife's constant advice was "Hang in there. Your boss is going to get fired." She genuinely thought her husband was the most brilliant man in the world and assumed that everyone else who mattered agreed. If the boss didn't, his days had to be numbered. So the man hung in there, waiting for the recognition his wife kept promising, which meant that he stayed much longer than appropriate, until the firm, finally accepting that he couldn't take a hint, fired him.

Tip: The one time to reach out is when you see the person you love truly suffering: if he or she is coming home with high blood pressure, or is drinking too much, or is in the throes of a deep depression. Then you support whatever options he or she is considering. You say, "If you hate this so much that it's hurting you, then a change is necessary, so let's talk about what we can do together."

Special advice for gay couples: Just because you're of the same sex doesn't mean that you share the same workplace values. For instance, a gay female I know, Betsy, ran into some prejudice on the job—she was taken off an account when her boss decided the client didn't like her. But Betsy hadn't enjoyed the account anyway, and she was happier with her new assignment, which the boss had hand-picked for her. Betsy's more politically minded partner, however, was furious, demanding that Betsy raise the possibility of legal recourse because homophobia was obviously involved. So Betsy did. The boss, in turn, was livid, and although Betsy abandoned the legal action, their once-genial relationship never quite recovered.

━✦ The Evil Twin on spouses: Often—perhaps too often—spouses become involved in office politics, and soon your spouse, the boss's spouse, your enemy's spouse, and all the other spouses are socially connected one way or another.

One common Evil Twin strategy is to turn the spouse into a communications tool. I knew one man whose wife was great friends with the CEO's wife; he used that friendship to pass along information that he didn't feel he could relay himself.

For instance, at a point when he was worried about his children's college education, he encouraged his wife to share their anxieties with her girlfriend, Mrs. CEO. Mrs. CEO not only got the message but passed it along, and rumor has it that this explained my friend's new raise.

Note: You can accomplish this only with a spouse who understands subtlety. If your spouse is the type who would like to give the CEO a piece of her mind, keep Spouse far away.

WITCH DOCTORS

In general, consultants show up at your company because the Big Boss has a nagging feeling in his gut. He knows something's wrong, he needs some kind of help, he doesn't know where to find it. He's probably shared his symptoms with someone he trusts, who in turn told him that when he himself felt similarly, he hired the Witch Doctor to cure him. So here comes the Witch Doctor, and he's not necessarily there to help you.

Be careful around consultants. The consultant's primary job is to say he's found a problem: So-and-So is flawed, such-and-such doesn't work. As a result of these troubles, he'll need to stay around longer, so he can bill more hours.

To locate these problems, consultants have to know what's going on inside and out at your company, and this means sucking everything out of employees' brains like a vacuum cleaner.

Good consultants are like therapists: They provide a secure atmosphere in which to talk openly. It often feels as if they care about you and your ideas—"You're one of the few people here who knows what she's talking about," the consultant confides. He's only said this to ten other people. That same morning.

Choose your words carefully. For instance, if the consultant gives you a chance to hurt your enemy, don't bite. I did once, and I lost. Many years ago a Witch Doctor asked me about an irritating colleague: "Is Ned strategic?"

"No," I answered. "Once Ned has his orders, he's excellent, but otherwise he's hopeless."

It didn't take long for the consultant to mention this comment to someone else, who told someone else, who told Ned, who then spent years calculating his revenge.

Consultants aren't about making you look good; they're about making themselves look good. Be careful not to open up vulnerabilities to them. If you have doubts, address them elsewhere.

—⬦ The Evil Twin on consultants: If you're really good, and I mean *really* good, you can use consultants to plant information. The consultant comes around asking for information about the X Project, which doesn't specifically involve you, but if there's another project that you feel could use some discouragement, you mention, casually, that while X seems to be going well, you've been hearing terrible things about Y Project. A good consultant is an information magnet, and your opinion may somehow find its way to a place where it won't help. As always, just make sure to keep your motives clean.

You can also get a better picture of what your boss was looking for when he hired this particular Witch Doctor. What isn't working at your organization? Is the consultant's mandate basically a cost-cutting exercise? Is it about market share? You can't look too curious, but you can try to trap the consultant into giving away information.

Some consultants allow their egos to get the better of them when it comes to I-know-more-than-you-do. You say, too smartly, "I know why you're here. It's that budget issue." A weak Witch Doctor replies (with luck), "That shows what you know. I'm tracking down a market share problem." However, if you do manage to get information out of him, be careful what you do with it. You don't want an angry Witch Doctor casting spells on you.

Bad Moon Rising

(There's Trouble on the Way . . .)

COVERING YOUR BUTT
DO THE RIGHT THING
ENEMIES: A LOVE STORY
FOR WHOM THE BELLS TOLL
FULL FRONTAL REVENGE
FUTURE SHOCK
GROVELING IN MORTIFICATION
IN SICKNESS AND IN WEALTH
THE SOUR GRAPES OF WRATH
STICKS AND STONES
THAT'S NO WAY TO SAY GOOD-BYE

COVERING YOUR BUTT

It's unfortunate, it's unpleasant, it's time-consuming—but there's no getting around it: Sometimes you just have to cover your butt.

Let's say your boss is up to something that makes neither sense nor money, and if you don't act your team is in trouble. But before you run for cover, conduct your own personal systems check. Is it possible that alarm you hear is your own personal hobbyhorse being activated? Half the time it may well be; all of us possess the capacity for self-righteousness and moral indignation.

But let's say this time it's for real. You've cross-examined your motivation and you're convinced there's cause for legitimate concern. Even though your boss may well be the source of the problem, she's the first place you go to seek help. Make sure, however, that your approach is so low-key that she doesn't feel threatened. A scared boss can wreak as much mindless destruction as a scared horse, stomping everything underfoot.

Murmur soothingly about good ideas that will fix the situation. Then let go of them by saying, "Of course, you've probably thought of all this," so she can approach her own boss and present the ideas as hers. Whenever you can prevent your boss from doing something stupid, you win. **If it makes your boss look good, it makes you look good.**

But perhaps the boss continues to resist. If the problem is so severe that there's no way to avoid addressing it, then you have to protect yourself. With luck, this shouldn't happen too often. But if you were working on a special project for the space shuttle, for instance,

and you knew your company's product was defective, you'd do anything necessary to release that information before the next launch.

When you do take action, store dated memos in the files. Write
down, "Here's this idea that would correct the problem." Keep a
hard copy. Don't mention anything about the boss's reaction; just
make it clear that you presented it to the boss and it went nowhere.

Sometimes, if you have the right access, you can talk to people
in other parts of the organization and make sure that they realize
you're in the know about a potential problem spot. But be careful.
Don't look as if you're squealing. Disguise your conversation. If
it's someone you're comfortable with, present your concern, for example, by talking about how work is getting you down, no one
appreciates you, you've been working around the clock—and by the
way, you had this great idea but your boss won't act on it. Your friend
will react to your complaints, and it may be some time before he
thinks about the rest of what you said, since you've made this part
seem incidental.

Don't be transparent. **Transparency creates enemies.** If
you manufacture a situation in which all you're doing is covering
your butt instead of attending to the company's best interests, you'll
make everyone angry. Likewise, don't send a cover-your-butt memo
to a big distribution list if that's the memo's only purpose. People will
understand what you're doing and resent it. They'll know right away
that it's nothing more than an attempt to save your own skin.

And don't cover more than you need to. Otherwise you run the
risk of either drawing people's attention to a problem they might not
otherwise see or making more of a mess. It's like a pimple: Sometimes the worst thing you can do is cover it with too much gunk; it
only draws attention to the flaw. The odds are that others might not
have even noticed it.

I've scrambled to cover my own butt many times, and many
of those attempts were unsuccessful. I remember once writing a

confirming memo about cutting funding for systems that I knew shouldn't have been cut. In the memo I cautioned that down the road these cuts would only create some real problems. But when those problems eventually did arise, having the memo in the files only made me look ineffectual. After all, I'd foreseen these problems, as the memo clearly stated, but didn't have the power to do anything about it.

Remember: They won't always remember that you were right, but they will remember if you were pathetic.

━✦ The Evil Twin on shifting blame: There's only one correct course of action when you see the possibility of taking the fall for no fault of your own: **Make sure that the people who need to know something know.** The Evil Twin knows how to do this without leaving tracks.

For instance, a friend of mine was the assistant director of sports marketing at a large Colorado department store. When her boss started submitting dishonest reports, Janet knew that if she confronted her boss, he'd fire her. So every time she received the fudged numbers, she'd make copies, put them in an envelope without a cover note, and send them to the legal department. She never discussed her discovery with anyone, but when the money people started to take a closer look at her boss's little fictions, they had what they needed to resolve any mysteries quickly.

DO THE RIGHT THING

Unlike Kansas in the film version of *The Wizard of Oz*, the world isn't black and white; life's issues are often much more complicated than a business school ethics instructor might lead you to believe. There may be no simple answers to questions such as: Is your boss cheating? Is your company committing a crime? What may seem like a violation to you may actually fall within the bounds of that particular industry's unwritten ethical code.

Nonetheless, there are times when clearly unethical activities take place. And when they do, good person that you are, you'll have to decide whether or not to blow the whistle.

A few years ago Doug, the highest-ranking African-American in his division at a Fortune 500 company, was having problems with his boss, who was acting strangely. She was taking employees, male and female, to lunch and asking them if they'd ever had extramarital sex. If the answer was yes, she asked them to describe their transgressions in detail. She also wanted to know who they fantasized about, particularly if it was someone at the office, and whether or not they were straight or gay.

Most of her employees laughed off these lunches or dismissed them as part of a peculiarly aberrant management style. But Doug, horrified, decided the company higher-ups would want to be notified.

What he discovered: This was the last thing the company wanted. They told him he was overreacting. They told him he was causing trouble. They told him they'd have to transfer him to a dif ferent department. All in all, they made it clear that Doug's news was not welcome.

A few notes on whistle-blowing:

Don't assume your company wants to hear from you. They may believe they do, they may even have an official policy that says they do, and they'll tell you they do. But for the most part, they don't.

These problems, particularly if they involve ethical concerns, are too difficult for the average bureaucracy. As is *not* the case with legal issues, the nature of ethics isn't cut and dried, and the subject can lead to a good deal of dissension and unpleasantness.

Ethical issues can also reflect a change in perception: What was okay yesterday isn't okay today. Top management often doesn't understand that behavior that was acceptable during their climb to the top over the last few decades isn't anymore. Don't expect your grievances to fall on open ears and minds.

You will probably take the hit. This is unfair. Life is unfair. Doug's fantasy that the company honchos would reward him for stopping a problem before it blew up was just that: a fantasy. Instead, they transferred him, they bad-mouthed him, and eventually they forced him out. There's a reason everyone talks about killing the messenger: History is littered with dead messengers.

If the story goes outside the company, it's out of your hands and therefore out of control. When this happens, your company suffers at the hands of the press—and possibly the stockholders. In Doug's case, the story blew up when a newspaper reporter heard about it and wrote a feature. Even then, Doug's boss wasn't fired, but the company suffered some humiliating press coverage.

I'm not advocating that you walk away from misdeeds. Blowing the appropriate whistle can be the proudest moment of your life. But be realistic. If you have to blow that whistle, and you're not protected by a strong mentor, be ready to leave once the whistle's been sounded. Powerful and paranoid factions will assume you're leaving anyway, and they will treat you as the enemy. If you try to stay, they'll try to destroy you.

Search your soul. Be clear about what personal baggage you're carrying—there's a good chance the issue at hand holds a special meaning for you that your opponents will quickly identify and use against you. If you've got a family member who died of lung cancer, and you're going after a tobacco company, they'll uncover this. Understand the cost. Talk to an attorney. Act like a scout: Be prepared.

The Evil Twin on whistle-blowing: Don't let your Evil Twin become involved in ethical matters. Never blow a whistle because you're angry at someone, or because you're the only person in your department who didn't get a raise, or because you're in a bad mood. Whistle-blowing is not an act of revenge. It's not an act of rage. It's an act of serious significance that will change your life and the lives of everyone around you, possibly forever.

ENEMIES: A LOVE STORY

If you're doing it right, you'll always have at least a few enemies at the office, although you may not know it at the time, and you may not be able to identify them all. How you deal with these enemies is as important as how you interact with your friends.

Surprisingly, you can get more accurate information from an enemy than from a friend. Friends shade the truth to protect you, **but when your enemies talk, listen.** Value your enemies for their candor.

For instance: One of my former co-workers, Edgar, had a great many detractors because he came across as pompous, to the point of being insufferable. At meetings, the moment his mouth opened, all eyes rolled. Edgar had some great qualities, too, but he was so long-winded no one ever discovered them. Eventually we found out that Edgar's first career was teaching, which explained why he talked to us as though we were students in his elementary school class. None of his friends would tell him that; how could we?

Finally, one of Edgar's most ardent detractors lost it and pointed out mid-drone that Edgar was always lecturing, goddammit, and no one needed to be talked to like that. The light dawned, a little, and Edgar started to work on his speech.

Your enemies are the ones who can help you change what you need to change. They'll brutally point out your flaws, but what they say is often more on target than your friends' observations.

Another gift from enemies: They identify your hot buttons. We all like to think that we're well protected at the office, but then, from out of nowhere, an enemy causes us to lose our cool in front of the boss just by pointing out a fashion flaw/asking where that accent came from/not laughing at a joke. We all have buttons, but we often don't know where they're hidden.

Enemies know our flaws better than we do. They know how to locate those buttons. Be grateful. Once these buttons have been pushed, you can shield them from future attacks.

There are times, however, when your enemies attack more than just your buttons and you need to withstand a barrage of unfriendly fire.

There are several ways to go. One of the best ways is by admitting vulnerability.

Your soft spots are the first places enemies target when they want to hurt you—but they can't get there if you get there first. If writing is your major weakness and you're willing to say, "I'm not good at writing reports, which is why I let Sally do it for me," you've left no opening for your enemies to attack. They can't say, "He has to make Sally write for him." You've already made that clear—and, in fact, you can also make it clear that you don't want to write. You're too busy and have too many other important duties.

These admissions of vulnerability can also be turned into a useful bridge to a potential enemy. Like many women of my generation, I suffer from math anxiety. In a stressful situation I can't add two and two, and as a result, some of Prudential's field managers found it easy to undercut me. All they had to do was wait for a big meeting and then ask me a hypothetical question that involved doing mental calculations in my head.

One guy specialized in this, rattling me until it was embarrassing for everyone. Finally I took him aside at a coffee break and said,

"We both know I'm terrible at numbers, and everyone knows you're good. But the truth is that I'm so bad, and you're so good, it makes you look bad when you pick on me. So if there really is a problem, talk to me outside the meeting and we'll fix it. And I'll make sure that the Boss knows you've been a big help in getting the project done."

What could he say? He never did it again.

Tip: When you make enemies, be careful. **Fighting with someone lower in status demeans you.** If you engage in such fights, your enemy suddenly seems powerful, since you're expending so much energy on him.

—⚡ The Evil Twin on enemies: As the old saying goes, the enemy of my enemy is my friend. If someone you're battling has an egregious enemy, it's easy for you to join forces with that person to form a strategic alliance. But be reasonable. You don't want all your allies to be your enemies' enemies.

My favorite tactic when it comes to enemies: Help them. You can kill with kindness; I've done it often with great success. Get them better jobs. Recommend them to other division heads. Give their names to headhunters and ease them into more powerful positions elsewhere. The best part: Not only are your enemies gone, but someday they'll find out what you did for them, and that will confuse them no end.

Still another maneuver: Encourage an enemy to go after an opponent who's in a higher weight class. If your rival Grant is a light-heavyweight, as well as an ambitious sort who doesn't know his own considerable limits, encourage him to go after a heavyweight. Let's say the Big Boss wants to keep the South American plant alive. "But, Grant," you tell him, "you know closing down Brazil is the only option. You can't just sit on your hands while it bleeds us dry. Go do something about it."

Grant listens to you, Grant decides to enter the ring with the Big Boss. Then, after he's carried out of the ring on a stretcher, you can walk behind him, shaking your head sadly.

FOR WHOM THE BELLS TOLL

It's those little chimes that signify trouble.

If you want to know how well you're doing, pay close attention to the scenery and you'll see signs—or hear chimes—everywhere. You walk into an office to talk to an associate who's on the phone. Does she get off the phone immediately? Does she signal you to stay but keep talking?

Different calibrations of this scene tell you all you need to know. If you're hot, she'll stop whatever she's doing to talk—or, if for some reason she can't, her distress will be visible. But if she continues her conversation, that means she doesn't think she needs to talk to you. And if you notice a similar shift in this pattern with others, you're in trouble.

Whenever people no longer seem to cooperate with you, whenever the system seems sluggish, pay attention. Sometimes it can indicate that the system is down, but often it means that you are.

Another place to look for signs is at meetings, where interruptions are omens. Normally only certain people get interrupted. For instance, no one cuts in on the boss. From there on down it's all fair game, since interruptions are a way to claim territory. If you're constantly being interrupted in meetings, that means everyone thinks they can trespass into your territory. The bell is tolling loudly.

Still one more sign: These days most people are fairly aware of body language, and you won't see too many people giving away their feelings by sitting through an entire meeting with their arms crossed.

But few people know how to manage their breathing. They feel antagonistic and they start snorting quietly or breathing too quickly. Few people can, or do, control changes in breathing patterns, and even fewer people know to look for them. Try it.

A Hollywood studio exec once knew he was out of a job due to a change in his view. One of his office walls was made entirely of glass, and other employees had to walk past it in order to reach the cafeteria—the only other route was a circuitous path around the other side of the building, which took several more minutes to travel and involved passing through extra doors. One week the man noticed that fewer and fewer senior executives were walking past his office, which meant that they were taking the longer route to eat, which in turn indicated that they didn't want to look at him. The subtle hint: They knew he was on the way out. His walking papers arrived a week later.

Tip: When you start hearing bells in the distance, you may want verification that you're sliding. That can be tough to obtain because your slide hasn't reached the acknowledgment stage. One extreme option: Force an innocent confrontation. Ask your boss, "Is everything working out? And can we talk about it?" You already know they don't want to talk about it, or they would have done so openly. But now you've put the ball in play, creating a situation where, although you'll probably lose, at least you'll confirm your suspicions and be prepared for the next step.

A note on too many tolling bells: Being fired is a milestone in almost everyone's career. It doesn't mean your employer is evil, which you'll probably think during the day, or that you're inadequate, which you'll be thinking in the middle of the night. It just means that something you were doing (or maybe something bigger than you, like your company) wasn't working. Being fired gives you the opportunity to learn what was going wrong, and how to change it, so you don't repeat history.

A final note: If you've never been fired, you may feel inclined to pat yourself on the back, but the reality in today's economy is that you're probably playing your career too safe. It's like having all your investments in CDs. No risk means no gain. Remember: Just because you haven't been fired doesn't mean that you're going to advance.

⟶⟵ The Evil Twin on the little things: Although most people don't pay overt attention to the scenery, their subconscious is usually in overdrive, making notes and sending odd signals to the conscious mind. You can make someone crazy by doing something as apparently insignificant as taking a day to return a call, particularly if he's accustomed to an immediate response. Or let him stand in your office a little too long while you're on the phone. Or, in midconversation, stop looking at his eyes and focus your vision elsewhere. Within seconds he'll be thinking, "Why isn't he looking at me? What did I do?"

FULL FRONTAL REVENGE

The basic objective of good office politics is to be afforded the chance to contribute your best efforts. If you can't do that, your product won't appear, your design won't be accepted, your report won't get disseminated. Whatever it is that expresses your talent won't see fruition if you and your peers don't play on the same team.

That's why revenge is almost always a bad idea. Rather than creating a good environment for good work, **revenge only succeeds in making a mess.** It's a distraction, it wastes time and energy, and it creates enemies, among them enemies you won't even recognize—a dangerous kind.

An incident: About five years ago three women at a Detroit telecommunications company lunched together and discovered something they'd all secretly suspected: They hated their boss, an assistant-bullying, idea-stealing, money-grubbing, irritable man without redeeming qualities.

The women decided that enough was enough, and they launched a revenge strategy. Over the next few months each of them filed a sexual harassment case against the man, using each other as witnesses. Because one of them had a legal background, their case was skillfully prepared; by the end of the year the boss was dismissed for cause.

But the story didn't end here. One of the women couldn't keep her mouth shut, and one night, a little drunk at the office's favorite neighborhood pub, she confided the truth to a co-worker, who swore it would go no further, which it didn't—until the next day. Word soon crept around the office, and seen in this new light, the harassment suit now looked like a conspiracy. Another of the women confessed. All three were fired.

Even worse: The ex-boss got wind of the story, whereupon he filed a wrongful dismissal suit against the company, which was forced to pay him a huge settlement.

The bottom line: The boss was a bad manager, but all the plotters accomplished was to bankroll his retirement and lose their jobs.

Some people think that the one time they can get away with revenge is when they're fired. Wrong. Revenge is messy even when you're on the way out.

One of the nastiest stories I ever heard took place at a large software company, where Elaine, the unpleasant, irascible head of marketing, and Jerry, the head of sales, were married. But Elaine was also having an affair with Jerry's number-two guy, which Jerry didn't know—but which Elaine's assistant, George, did. George also knew how impossible Elaine was to work for, and sure enough, one day Elaine worked herself up into a gratuitous rage and fired George, who then took all the E-mail Elaine and her boyfriend had been trading—and which George had been assiduously saving—and sent it throughout the entire firm. End result: Elaine was fired, but George never got another job in the industry. Word of the story spread faster than a virus, and no one wanted to hire anyone capable of such enraged retribution.

⚡ The Evil Twin on revenge: Proceed with caution. Unless you're totally, completely, absolutely backed into a corner, walk away. But if you have no other choice, bear in mind that the only revenge strategies that work are the ones where you don't get caught. And since you have no guarantee of this, I don't recommend revenge.

Are there no exceptions?

Only if the revenge is not only well deserved but truly well managed. Remember, I'm assuming that everyone who's reading this book is basically a good person who listens to the Evil Twin only when there's no other option. By definition, then, the person from whom you want revenge is a bad person—otherwise the situation wouldn't arise. Also by definition, chances are good that your enemy is up to no good, and he doesn't want anyone else to know. Well, perhaps other people should know. But don't reveal everything at once. Don't go for the jugular. **The death of a thousand cuts is more effective than an open stab to the heart.**

An Evil Twin revenge strategy: Most people worthy of revenge strategies have a nickname that arises from some genuine flaw, whether it's Space Man, Coma Baby, or, as one of my friend's arch-rivals was called, Hairball, referring to the man's constant ability to talk without ever bringing up anything attractive. So, say you're at a meeting with your boss and seemingly inadvertently you allow the name Hairball to slip into the conversation: "I think personnel is reporting directly on this to Hairball, oops, I mean Harry." The damage is done, your revenge complete. Your boss will never again look at Harry without thinking Hairball.

The most damaging nickname I ever heard involves Jake, a salesman promoted over other, more competent peers due to his close relationship with the boss, who also happened to be his brother-in-law. At the first meeting after the promotion was announced, when Jake left the room, someone started whistling the theme song from *The Andy Griffith Show.* "He's dumb as Barney Fife," she explained. From that moment on, whenever Jake left the room, everyone whistled his theme.

Evil Twin revenge strategies should be so fast and clean that the victim doesn't even notice until he walks out of his office and wonders whose blood is seeping over the carpet.

FUTURE SHOCK

If your boss isn't talking to you about your future, then you probably don't have one.

Most people obsess about their future. And they wonder why their employers don't. "What do you have to do to get them to talk about your career around here?" people grumble.

The problem is the common assumption that "they" have a great plan in store for you. "They" don't. It's a myth that the people above you are plotting your career path. They're plotting, all right, but the focus of their plots is their own careers.

Now, there are a very few people who've indeed been selected for advancement. These people are identified early on and are given significant opportunities. "Shelley," they say, "take over the southern territories, and if the results are good the rest is history." And Shelley's on her way.

But if no one's making this kind of speech to you, the odds are they never will, and there's not much you can do about it. Think of it in terms of love. Have you ever tried to make someone love you? Then you know how hard it is. You can't force your company to love you, either. Be reasonable about your future, and if you're so ambitious that you can stay at a job only if you think you have a good shot at running the whole place, and no one there seems to agree, think about running to some other place.

—⟡ The Evil Twin on the future: There are ways, however, to stack the deck—if and only if you have solid signs that they like you. Manipulate the light in which you're seen. For instance, if your boss doesn't think you have leadership skills, join a professional organization that allows you to work at that level and invite your boss over to witness your work. It's the old Miss-Jones-I-had-no-idea-you-were-so-beautiful-until-you-took-your-glasses-off-and-let-your-hair-down theme. And the best part is that not only have you remade your image, you've probably done some excellent work for a deserving volunteer cause, or you've made contacts that will help you find your next spot.

GROVELING IN MORTIFICATION

My husband, Jim, once had an employee who was as close to perfect as a human can get. Pamela was smart, talented, and beautiful. But, being mortal, she did possess one or two flaws, including a pathological need to handle more projects at one time than was possible—until the inevitable day came when she blew a client deadline. The client freaked, and Pamela knew that it wouldn't take long before he'd be on the phone to Jim, reaming him out for her lapse.

By the time Pamela met with Jim he was turning an unfortunate shade of red, which meant that the feared conversation had already taken place.

Pamela looked into Jim's eyes, speaking clearly and quietly. She said, "I grovel in mortification." End of speech.

Jim was not only charmed, he had discovered another aspect of Pamela's impeccability: the perfect understanding of when to cop to a mistake.

There are going to be times when you'll screw up, and when you do, the proper response is to grovel. Making excuses for your errors is unseemly, pathetic, and makes the offended party even angrier. **Take the blame; it's the only attractive response.**

When do you grovel? Whenever it's your responsibility, *responsibility* being defined as broadly as is reasonably possible. The company was counting on you, and you blew it. For whatever reason. It happens. Tell your boss you made a mistake and that you're sorry. Period. (But don't go overboard. If you go on too long and act too contrite, you'll come across as pompous. Remember what Golda Meir told a groveling opponent: "You're not important enough to be so humble.")

It's even appropriate to grovel if the mistake was part of a team error and the actual goof was someone else's. And if you're talking to a client or a customer, anything your company has done wrong is your fault, as far as they're concerned.

People who don't accept blame think that they're managing their self-image. They're not. Bosses aren't blind. The odds are pretty good that they know you're responsible. So if you make a mistake, don't point at your assistant. Maybe you'll get away with that once. But when it happens twice, it's a pattern, and it's one that makes you look foolish.

Many people have the misplaced notion that others are impressed when they get away with something: tax dodging, cheating on alimony, pirated cable access, and so on. But when someone brags about letting others take the blame for her mistakes, it leaves a lingering, queasy feeling in most people's stomachs.

For instance: At an office party a few years ago, Bud started talking about his teenage job: driving a loading cart in a brewery. The tale ended with him accidentally destroying many cases of beer and speeding off before anyone realized he was responsible. Bud thought it was funny. But it left me with unspoken questions about the poor soul who had to pay for the destruction out of his own pocket. And I wasn't the only one wondering; when Bud left the table, the man on my left looked at me and said, "What a jerk."

People will tell such a story because they think it makes them look smart. It doesn't. It's a boomerang that always comes back to hurt them.

Tip: Some people believe wholeheartedly in the popular Ostrich Maneuver: You've just screwed up, and your response is to stick your head below ground. Think about it. Maybe your head's now covered, but your butt's up in the air, unprotected. Neither smart not attractive.

—⚡ The Evil Twin on accepting blame: Whenever you're dealing with someone who can't accept responsibility graciously, back him into a dead end. You know he's not going to admit he was wrong. So push it.

For instance, Roz once worked with a somewhat overbearing, well-educated, otherwise well-adjusted middle-management-for-life type named Niles, who thought that everyone in the world was guilty of something, except him. Niles could pour a cup of coffee on your lap and manage to blame the waiter, the maitre d', and the cook, even though no one else was nearby when it happened. His idea of personal responsibility began with you and ended with everyone else.

All this never bothered Roz much until Niles started cozying up to the Boss in ways that indicated that he was trying to make a move. For reasons of his own, Niles turned himself into Roz's enemy—as well as several other people's. And due to the relentlessness of Niles's personality, he was an enemy everyone had to deal with. The solution: set Niles up.

This boss was a relatively decent fellow, but he didn't know Niles well, nor was he aware of Niles's blame-avoiding personality. So Roz had to let the Boss know about Niles's unpleasant foible in order to spare innocent people. But Roz didn't want to say it outright.

Instead, Roz waited for the appropriate opportunity, which appeared soon enough. The Big Guy had asked Niles to come up with some numbers by the following Monday. Niles didn't do it. So all Roz had to do was make sure that the Boss remembered that Niles had had sole responsibility for these numbers, which she did before Niles arrived Monday morning—late, of course, since his alarm clock was broken, the taxi driver got lost, his train was late.

Once that was done, Roz stepped back and let Niles do the rest. He arrived at 10 A.M. empty-handed. Those numbers? he asked. It wasn't his responsibility. It was Daphne's fault. It was Martin's fault. The Boss didn't believe any of this. And the more Niles protested, the worse he looked. And so ended Niles's brief fling at ambition.

IN SICKNESS AND IN WEALTH

Poor Hilda. She worked at a company where every year employees were given ten sick days, and every year Poor Hilda took off every one of those days. Bronchitis, sore throats, migraine headaches: Poor Hilda managed to contract them all.

The problem was that no one believed her. Poor Hilda was sick exactly ten days each and every year? Sure.

Don't deplete all your sick time. It sends the wrong message. Looking back over my career, I can remember the name of every subordinate who routinely used up every sick day. There weren't that many of them. They stood out.

I'm not saying you shouldn't be sick, and clearly major illnesses are another matter. But there are going to be plenty of days when it's a fifty-fifty decision: Your throat is scratchy, your fever's just slightly above normal, your head aches. The person who always says, "I just don't feel like it" is going to get the reputation as someone who's not motivated in other ways.

If you do decide to stay home, don't call in and say you have "just a little something." No one likes a sickness sissy. Nor should you try excuses such as "I got food poisoning." This works occasionally, but if you use it too often it's like saying your grandmother died again. Nor should you call in sick while sounding great. When you're truly ill, the call comes from someone else, along the lines of "Trip's too sick to make it to the office today," the unsaid message being "The poor slob can't even get to the phone."

On those days when you show up at the office sick, minimize it. Ostentatious sickness is a mistake. Offices aren't humane places; the basic rule is that you aren't supposed to show frailty. You're not even supposed to be human. CEOs don't brag about taking naps and living balanced lives. CEOs brag about how rarely they get sick or how little sleep they need. "I read ten books last week, which was easy to do since I'm awake twenty-two hours every day," they say. "I've never taken a sick day in my life, so I don't see any reason why anyone else should."

A Wall Street trader I know recently had bypass surgery. "Normally we don't get to see guys like you," his doctor said.

"Why?" the trader asked.

"Usually you guys just push away from the desk," the doctor replied, "say, 'I don't feel so good,' keel over, and die."

So when a ruthless influenza is sweeping through the office and the corridors are littered with empty bottles of aspirin, don't show off. Some people like to drape their desks with wet tissues, cough horribly, and surround themselves with steaming hot liquids. Wrong. And the more macho your work environment, the less cool it is to display your illness.

When you're sick, it feels good to have loved ones feel sorry for you. That's comforting. What you don't want is for co-workers to feel sorry for you. That's dangerous.

Then there's major illness, which the workplace doesn't understand. Having a long-term sickness is an unfortunate fact of life for some, but don't count on the office to be there for you. Human Resources will have told everyone to be nice, but they won't necessarily rise to the occasion—sickness means you're unpredictable, which, as has been discussed, is the worst-case scenario for politics. The only thing you can do is give out as little information as possible, and manage your self-image as well as possible. If you can, work out a situation where you take on less responsibility. Too many people become ill and tell themselves they can handle it. Too often they can't, and their bosses never quite forget.

There is one acceptable serious illness, because all tough guys expect to experience it someday, and because it indicates that you've been working too hard: the heart attack. Guys like to bond over it: "What was it like?" "How did it happen?" and the unspoken but intimated, "How close did you come to buying the farm?"

Tip: Road warriors are more likely to be sick than anyone else. Air travel is like taking a dip in a bath of microbes. Assume that people who travel are sick, even if you they tell you they're not. They're so used to being sick they don't notice it. Be careful around them. They're not at their best and they need extra attention.

Special Tip: To put it bluntly, the workplace is dysfunctional when dealing with death. This derives from a general lack of ability in our society to handle mourning, and also from the macho sensibility that pervades the office. A few years ago a co-worker lost his sister unexpectedly and took a day off. When he returned to the office, I told him I was sorry. "Yeah," he said. "What did I miss?" And that was the end of the discussion.

"Yeah." That's all. That's what it's suppose to be like. Someone you love dies, and as far as the office is concerned, you're supposed to be tough. The problem is that grieving lasts longer than a day.

The bottom line: **Accept that you're not going to receive much support for grieving at the office.** Lower your expectations. You'll get a lot of notes and nice cards, but that's probably all you'll get. Death is such an intimate occurrence, touching the deepest core of our being, that most people prefer to avoid it. So find the few people you truly care for and lean on them when you need sustenance. And you never know: Someone you've never paid much attention to may be the one who provides you the most support, maybe because he or she has suffered a similar experience and knows exactly what you're going through.

Bosses who know how to handle death can inspire enormous loyalty among their employees. I was devastated by my own father's death, but I knew enough not to bring it to the office. On my first day back, however, my boss had instructed the security guards to alert him when I entered the building, and when I arrived in my office he was waiting for me, and he spent the next half hour sympathizing. From that moment on I'd have done anything for him.

Caution: The office handles death badly, but it doesn't handle pet death at all. Although I love pets as much as anyone, I don't show my bosses pictures of my cats and I don't involve co-workers when they die. I once saw a woman's career end after her incessant grieving over Mr. Ruffles; first she took five days off from work, and then she spent the next few months talking about Mr. Ruffles every possible moment.

If your Mr. Ruffles dies, find the one other person in your office who has the same kind of pet and grieve with that person—and only with that person. Privately.

For women only: Maternity leave is perfectly acceptable as long as you handle it perfectly. I can't make any blanket statements regarding the appropriate wording and timing of your announcement, but I can advise you to play it close to the vest until absolutely necessary. You have to use your own judgment, but do weigh all the variables before you decide how to spring the good news—who you tell first, when you tell, and so on. Don't expect everyone else to be sincerely thrilled. For many, your happy news translates into three months of extra work and aggravation—for them.

⚔ The Evil Twin on illness: Anyone who takes advantage of anyone else's illness in any way is just evil.

THE SOUR GRAPES OF WRATH

Hate is hateful. It wears everyone down, it gets in the way of work, it sucks up energy, it destroys egos. It's what makes an ordinary bad day a truly bad day.

At any given time, if you're lucky, no one important will hate you. But like love, hate is irrational, so you never know when it's going to appear, or why, or where. Still, the odds are good that it will.

Few people handle hate well. During the course of my career I've seen too many adults fall into that terrible tail-biting circle where two people run around, nipping at each other's heels until the situation explodes and they revert to childish behavior, stalking out of meetings if the other walks in, refusing to speak to the other's friends, making fun of each other in public. Ridiculous behavior— but it doesn't seem so to the people involved. Their hatred, so all-consuming, devours their better judgment.

The most important thing to remember about hate: **Even when you're sure someone hates you, the odds are good you're wrong.** Often what we interpret as hate is only the daytime drama of normal neuroses and insecurities being played out in the office.

The kind of irrational hate that gets started back in childhood is the most difficult to deal with. Maybe that guy over there loathes you because you have blond hair and blue eyes—or because you don't. Or because you're thin, or because you're fat. Or because you went to prep school, or because you didn't go to prep school.

Hate, which feeds on our deepest fears about ourselves, starts when we're young. By the time we're grown this hate is in full flower, and work is its center stage because work is where we have the fewest choices about who we spend our time with.

Don't give in to the natural instinct to strike back. Since what you're fighting in these cases isn't hate, but inbred biases and prejudices, it has little to do with you. You can't help it if you don't conform to someone else's vision of who you should be. The problem is his, not yours, and you don't have to personalize it.

Another major hate-related issue: the misinterpretation of other people's actions. I've seen too many people decide that someone hated them for such small details as not exchanging a greeting. For instance: Alice, an old assistant, came from the sort of family that freely kissed and hugged, and since Dinah, the office manager, never responded with more than a quick nod, Alice was convinced Dinah loathed her.

When this began to consume Alice, I had to pin Dinah down and question her. She was completely taken aback—she'd never noticed Alice's friendly overtures; it wasn't part of her landscape. If Alice had gone after her for this perceived slight, she would have made an enemy out of someone who had no intention of being one. Don't judge others on how they would react if they were you. They're not you, and they never will be.

Hating others can be more destructive than being hated.

If you find yourself overcome with loathing toward a co-worker, analyze what's going on before giving in to the impulse to declare him an enemy. Someone approaches your desk, looking unhappy; you can assume that he doesn't like you and doesn't want to be there, or you can assume he's distracted by an agenda that has nothing to do with you. You control the connection to the thought, "He doesn't like me."

Also: Whenever possible, form your own judgments. You move

to a new office and the buzz on the guy next door suggests that he's a bastard. Perhaps he is; perhaps he isn't. And even if it's true in someone else's opinion, it may not be the case for you. Plenty of times I've been warned that So-and-So was an all-around bad guy, only to find out that So-and-So was going through a personal crisis, or was feeling left out by everyone else, or simply didn't like to socialize.

Look carefully at the patterns of hate in your life. In my case, it took years to realize that my work aversions almost always revolved around sibling issues—the natural object of my hatred was, without fail, a colleague of approximately my age and station who became a sudden favorite with the Powers That Be. And even though I recognized this pattern, I still succumbed.

One woman who sticks in my mind was a very high-profile personality, the kind other people find delightful: charming, fun, high-spirited. I couldn't abide her. For the life of me I couldn't understand why others could, especially our boss, who was so smart about everyone else. Couldn't he see how silly she was, with her name-dropping, her social climbing, her flagrant compliments?

It was bothering me so much, I had to develop a coping mechanism. Late one night, desperate, I decided to minimize her power by creating a new mental picture of her—I imagined her as a nineteenth-century servant girl bowing obsequiously to the Lord Master. From then on, every time she irritated me I summoned up this image, which made me smile. This wasn't a permanent solution to my sibling issues, but at least I'd found a way to work with her.

An old friend has come up with another solution: He and his enemy say terrible things about each other in front of their staff, but they do it in a humorous tone of voice. Only they know that it's all true.

Tip: **Garden-variety hate is displayed several levels down the food chain.** The higher you go up the executive ladder, the more likely it is that people delegate their emotional work to underlings. If you're looking to see who hates whom at the top, don't watch the two executive vice presidents. They'll appear to get along. Watch their staff—if their staffs are at war, the executives are, too.

—⚡ The Evil Twin on hatred: Nothing brings out your Evil Twin like hate: "That person hates me, so therefore I'm justified in doing all sorts of terrible things to her."

Don't. The key to making the Evil Twin work for you is control. Remember: The first item on the Evil Twin Code of Honor is discipline. Precipitous action will hurt you more than the person you hate. Vengeance is not only best served cold, it's downright explosive when served hot (see Full Frontal Revenge).

Over the years I've come to realize that one of the most evil, and therefore the most satisfying, defense mechanisms is simply to acknowledge the other person's hate and not return it. Not only does this require less energy, it drives your enemy crazy.

But let's say you really hate someone and you have a logical, clearheaded reason to take her out. If you're going to do it, do it well. Be relentless. Embarrass her repeatedly—not by attacking her personally, but by attacking her ideas. One of the best places to do this is in meetings. You arrange this by running the meeting yourself or by getting someone close to you to do it.

Let's say you hate Tommy. Stack the meeting with people who share your position, or at least get to them first to explain your ideas fully. Then make your cause sound as clear and just as the day is long: "I'm in favor of doing X because I believe it's right for the client," you comment evenly, "while Tommy is in favor of doing Y." (The implication being that Y is anticlient.) "Tommy, would you take us through your position?" you say, courteous to a fault. But the implied message is, "Tommy is wonderful, but this idea, which happens to be Tommy's, is typically idiotic."

STICKS AND STONES

How you give and take feedback can color your day, not to mention your entire career.

Case in point: My friend Paul went into a meeting the other day, ostensibly to give his boss a progress report on an important company-wide project. But the real reason was to impress the Big Guy.

The assignment was a laborious task that no one in the company had ever gotten right, and Paul was doing the best job imaginable. So there he was, halfway through the meeting, conducting the department heads' little corporate tap dances, when the Big Boss interrupted one of them midtap. Looking straight at Paul, he said, "I don't understand. What are the priorities here? Clearly, we're not going to go around the room and listen to everyone."

Since this was exactly what Paul had in mind, and everyone knew it, everyone also knew the Big Boss had just slapped Paul upside the head.

Paul regrouped and protested. "Let's keep going," he said. "We need to get the broader perspective before we hone in on the specifics."

Wrong.

By fighting back, even weakly, Paul upset the Big Boss, who didn't expect anything but a sharp turn in his direction. He hadn't intended to hurt Paul; it was just a small slap to remind Paul not to waste his time. But now everyone else was upset, too.

When your boss decides, for whatever reasons, to give you a few lumps, the last thing you want to do is become defensive. Nor do you want to show that you're upset (see Put On a Happy Face.) Lumps are like those bites that pets give their owners, those nips that don't break the skin or draw blood but say "Pay attention!" The message is that whatever you were doing in the moment preceding the bite wasn't going over well. And as with pets, if you continue, you run the risk that the boss will become irritated enough to draw blood.

There's only one appropriate strategy: **When publicly attacked by the boss, surrender.** Big dog comes, big dog bites; do what puppies do—roll on your back and show your belly. "Yes, Boss," you're saying. "You win. You are indeed more powerful."

Paul's strategic response should have gone like this: "Boss, you're right. We have too much on the table, and the reason I invited everyone was so we can all get a better sense of your priorities. What would you say are the top three items on your agenda?"

Even if it sounds slightly obsequious, this kind of response will help you look as though you're still in control, so even though everyone in the room saw you get backhanded, you don't appear wounded. If you don't flinch, people will doubt their own perceptions. Maybe it wasn't a backhand, they think. Maybe it was something completely different. Maybe you really were trying to get feedback. Whatever the case, you don't fight with your boss in public as though you were an equal. You're not.

Taking lumps intelligently is difficult, but for many people taking praise is harder. They become embarrassed, they turn red, they discount the praise as though it were some gift they couldn't imagine keeping. Your boss says, "You did a fine job on those numbers," and you respond, "No I didn't, it was just luck. Anyway, did you see where I ran into trouble on page 461a?"

All wrong. The boss probably didn't know you'd goofed. And you're making him feel bad for having complimented you.

The best response to praise: Accept it, then return it. "You did a good job here," says Boss. "Thanks," you say. "I appreciate it. But it helped that you told me how to get this part done."

The more inclusive you can make the praise, the better. The boss has thrown out some good vibes; your job is to take those vibes and increase them, so the whole room vibrates in praise.

Another excellent response is the *Bull Durham* approach. In that film, Kevin Costner's character gave this advice to his arrogant young pitcher about talking to the media: **Tell them you're just glad to play for the team.** This kind of response not only lends you an air of humility, it gives you the opportunity to go back to the team and tell them the Big Boss is proud of everyone, and so are you. The more people you can include, the better.

When you receive personal praise, don't take it upon yourself to spread it around: "Hey! Big Boss thinks I'm a god." If you feel it's necessary to get a piece of praise out on the grapevine, restrict yourself to the one or two people who really like you and let them do the talking.

One category of worker every supervisor knows is the Sub Rosa Sniveler, who passes along flattering memos others have written about him. "Dear Gus," the note says. "You're the best. If it weren't for you, this project would have tanked." Then Gus forwards it with a note saying, "Boss, isn't this guy terrific?"

Maybe, but Gus is a jerk. The only notes to pass along involve the performances of your subordinates and team members. It's fine to be proud of your people, and you create a nice moment when you and Big Boss can quietly bask in the glow together.

──❖ The Evil Twin on feedback: Fake feedback takes the form of abject flattery. The Evil Twin's praise sows the seeds of self-destruction: "It was great the way you told off that guy," says the Twin to someone who needs to learn to keep his mouth shut. "I admire the way you seize the opportunity," says the Twin to a grabby, overaggressive peer. Or, "You're a terrific writer. Send out more stuff like this," said to someone who can't write a simple sentence. In other words, say anything that keeps your enemy from noticing a blind spot.

THAT'S NO WAY TO SAY GOOD-BYE

One of my colleagues, Chuck, recently left his job. Chuck is a good man; honest, hardworking, and well liked. But Chuck had some bad luck when a new boss was brought in from outside and they couldn't get along. It wasn't anyone's fault, it wasn't planned, no one had it in for Chuck. It was simply a case of the wrong men put together at the wrong time.

Chuck then self-destructed. When he left the company, he told everyone how unhappy he was. He made sure that anyone friendly with his boss felt his fury. He insinuated that friends had betrayed him. He yelled at his assistant for staying behind. He refused to say good-bye to most of his co-workers.

No one blamed Chuck. We all knew he was hurting and that some of what he said was true. But the truth wasn't important. What mattered was that Chuck's behavior was so unseemly that everyone's last recollection of him was as a loser.

Chuck then went off on his own, and now he's calling people, asking for work. But no one wants to answer those calls.

Depart with style. The exit door is not the place to vent frustrations. It's a freeze-frame, the last moment people will see you, and you want them to remember you in the best possible light. Even if you've been truly wronged, it does no good to explode.

—⟶ The Evil Twin on exit doors: If Chuck had listened to his Evil Twin rather than his anger, he could have profited. Chuck knew that things weren't working out for him. He knew that no matter what transpired over the next few months, he was eventually going to have to leave. Instead of sulking, he should have been plotting.

Here's what he could have done. Chuck had always wanted to go off on his own and start a consultancy practice. But he never had the nerve to leave his salaried position, or enough money to cover those first few months before his clients paid up. Now, like it or not, he was being given the nudge out the door. The proper procedure would have been for his Evil Twin to pave the road to his new business.

First, Chuck should have employed strategy number one: Turn all the rules upside down. For instance, you normally don't allow rivals to make territorial incursions. But when you know you're toast, let it happen. Chuck should have allowed his empire to get so chipped away that there was little left. Then he should have gone to the Big Boss and let her come to the conclusion that Chuck, a good guy and a good worker, was no longer needed. After all, it was clear that others were doing the job quite well. Chuck, for the good of the company, was willing to sacrifice himself.

The Big Boss, feeling guilty, would have been inclined to assuage that guilt with a healthy severance package. And Chuck, instead of asking for handouts, would have had enough money to take care of those first few months on his own.

This was also the time for Chuck to break another rule. Normally you can't trust anyone with a secret. Chuck should have ignored this and slowly planted the seeds of knowledge about his new venture with several friends. Soon those close friends would have told everyone else, and instead of looking pathetic, Chuck would have repositioned himself as the guy who broke free to set up an exciting new business. Furthermore, by the time he'd gone, he'd have been able to drum up some business from friends who had spread the word throughout his industry.

Still another rule to break when you leave: Feuding may be good for office survival (see Hatfields and McCoys), but it's not good when you're facing the exit door. Even though Chuck hated Rhoda, the bean counter, as much as anyone else, now that he was leaving, it was the time to extend a glad hand to Rhoda. Chuck should have told her just how much he'd always admired the way she never let anyone touch her, and offered her a chance to cut a little off his budget before he left. After all, you never know when even Rhoda might be in a position to pass along some business.

Here, There,
and Everywhere

*(On the Phone, in the Bathroom,
on the Computer, at a Bar . . .)*

EDIFICE COMPLEX

ON THE ROCKS

PLANES, TRAINS, AND AUTOMOBILES

PRIVATE PARTS

SMOOTH OPERATOR

VIRTUAL POLITICS

YOU ARE WHERE YOU EAT

EDIFICE COMPLEX

Darren works in crisis management, which means he spends most of his life in airplanes, flying around the world to meet with whichever company is in the middle of a bankruptcy, a hostile takeover, or a public relations fiasco. Therefore Darren tends to see people when their firm's dirty details are leaving newsprint smudges all over America's hands. From these tense experiences he has gleaned many corporate truisms, perhaps the truest of which is that there's an inverse relationship between the size of the CEO's office and the talents of its occupant, or: **A huge office is usually an indication of a small-minded CEO.**

Real estate—and by that I mean offices—isn't just symbolic. It often reveals more about what's truly going on at the job than any official statement, annual report, or performance review. It can even matter more than money. You may be making $200 a week more than me, but as long as I don't know, it doesn't bother me. Even if I do, it still doesn't necessarily rankle if other people don't.

But if we're peers, and you've got a corner office with four windows while I'm parked in a small room with two windows, my stomach will turn somersaults. Why? **Your office is traditionally the most visible indicator of how much you're valued.** It's a concrete measure of how the company feels about you. You may think you're well-liked and well-respected, but if you've got the smallest office in a row of peers, something's going on.

Due to real estate's loaded symbolism, employers often use it to get rid of people they don't have solid grounds for firing.

One Los Angeles talent agency is notorious for yanking unwanted employees from large windowed offices and placing them in small cubicles, a real estate euphemism for "Get out." Even though these relocated agents know they're not being fired, the move is so demoralizing, they feel like the chosen in *The Lottery*: First they're shunned by their colleagues, and then they die, not by stoning but through neglect.

I knew of one Big Shot who was a ruthless son of a bitch when it came to his outside competition, but staff matters turned him into such mush, he couldn't bear to fire a soul. So instead of confronting employees directly, he played with real estate. First, he moved a victim down the hall. Then down another hall, or maybe onto another floor. Once the man moved a senior executive's office over and over until she landed on a floor where the firm had no other offices, the corporate equivalent of Siberia.

Some companies, especially ones that sell office furniture or rent space, continually invent miracle cures for the politics of office geography: cubicles, open architecture, inverted pyramids. They rarely work.

A Florida manufacturing firm tried running the office in what's known as Hotel Style. Each day, employees had to grab any available office, which denied them the chance to claim space as their own. Theoretically, this practice should stop invidious comparisons. But the employees rose up in revolt, since no one likes living in a hotel full-time (unless housekeeping and room service are provided).

Likewise, the CEO of a major airline once designed his own office as a cube in the middle of the first floor. But then everyone else in the company wanted to be in the middle of the floor in a cube, too, to prove that they were important also.

There's very little you can do if you're unhappy about office real estate. Unlike in your home, you can't call in a contractor to build an addition or knock down a wall. And there are some things you should never do. Above all, never complain to your peers. That only makes you look powerless. They already know about your inadequate space. It's up to you to pretend there isn't a problem.

Remember: It could always be worse. When a large communications company recently relocated, every employee was assigned a new office according to a salary code. A couch and a window meant a salary over $100,000, a cubicle without an easy chair meant less than $25,000, and so on. There were clearly six levels of real estate fortunes displayed, and therefore, within minutes of starting their first day in the new office, every person in the company now knew everyone else's salary range.

—⚡ The Evil Twin on real estate: Point out the obvious without saying a word. When someone you detest is downgraded to a smaller space, smile knowingly, insinuating the full weight of what you hope everyone knows the move must mean.

If the opposite has happened—your rivals score big offices and you don't—ask leading questions. "Do you honestly think Fred's ready for this?" you wonder aloud; or "I wonder if Lucy can handle the new load?"—implying that somehow you know he's not and she can't. This isn't much, but it beats stewing in your cubicle.

I've also seen people in hip computer-related jobs try the large-office-as-anachronism approach. When your rival lands a superior piece of real estate, show off your new super laptop. Say that you're into being close to the client/market and, anyway, you can't understand why these old Neanderthals prefer their large caves.

ON THE ROCKS

It's been a long, rough day, and now it's late in the evening; you're tired, you're worn, you're beat, but you just don't feel like going home. So when a few of your co-workers suggest that you all go out to everyone's favorite bar for a drink, you're delighted.

Don't be. **There's got to be a morning after.** When people drink, their inhibitions recede and fanciful new ideas pop into their heads. Co-workers who never dreamed of touching each other now fantasize that they look like movie stars—sort of—and they can't believe they never touched each other before—or did they?—and it's time to remedy the situation—more or less. . . .

Act under the influence and you'll regret it when you're over the influence. Maybe not the next day, or the next, but a week, a month, or a year later: You never know when it will come back to haunt you. But it will. Most of the harassment cases I've heard of developed because consensual relationships bloomed over a seemingly innocent consensual cocktail.

Alcohol affects people in strange ways, which has been true ever since humans started drinking, and these strange ways defy prediction. We all know that sexual appetites can be whetted, as well as memories destroyed. The problem is that's only for starters.

My friend Rob once worked for a woman who was the essence of composure at the office. Laura ran her division cleanly and efficiently, like one of those advertisements for nuclear power. One night after work, Rob and Laura went out for a bite to eat, and it came out during their conversation that it was Laura's birthday, whereupon Rob insisted on ordering a bottle of champagne. Laura put up a fight, but her loneliness got the best of her, and soon she'd downed several glasses.

It wasn't long before Rob was attracted to Laura, who'd become alluring in the way that someone who's always buttoned up can become when a few of those buttons come loose. But Rob never got to first base. Instead, Laura turned chatty about their office mates. Sally, she confided, was a bitch; Buddy couldn't carry his weight; Allan should have been fired years ago; and that was just the beginning. But before Laura got weepy over life's injustices, she managed to pull herself together and went home, alone.

The next day, when Rob spotted Laura at the water cooler, he expected to continue their newly formed friendship. Instead, she froze him out—and she continued to do so in the months that followed. Eventually, Rob transferred to another department. Laura had been so mortified by what she'd said that she didn't know what else to do. It wasn't the smartest or the most humane way to deal with what she considered to be an embarrassing moment of personal confession. But she was the boss, and she did what she did to cope.

Tip: The abuse factor in recreational drugs is just as dangerous, and since drugs are illegal, you're even more vulnerable. I've heard too many sad stories to count: Two young friends sharing a joint and then failing a new assignment's drug-screening test; a onetime cocaine snort with an unstable colleague who falsely claimed more followed; a well-meaning co-worker trying to coax a friend into rehab, and the entire company finding out. Point: Drugs don't belong at the office.

—⟡ The Evil Twin on alcohol: Another reason to be very careful when drinking with workmates is that you never know if you're really drinking with their Evil Twins. All it takes is a few cocktails, and that attractive young assistant of yours is suddenly looking at you with admiring eyes, telling you how wonderful you are, how sexy you are. And then, by the way, how hard it is to make ends meet on such a small salary . . . and the next thing you know, you've promoted a twenty-three-year-old assistant to vice president.

PLANES, TRAINS, AND AUTOMOBILES

It's a cold, cold winter in the North; the temperatures are low, the snow is high, and everyone's got the flu. Most of your firm's work takes place in the immediate area, but there's one account in Hawaii. And now there's trouble in Honolulu. Someone has to get on a plane. The boss picks you.

Q: Do you kick up your heels in joy? Sway through the halls with your ukulele? Or groan bitterly about having to leave the office?

A: Groan. **Whenever you travel, act as though it's a burden, particularly when it isn't.**

And bear that burden like a carry-on suitcase: with ease. Your demeanor says, "It's a tough job but someone's got to do it, and I'm tough, so it might as well be me."

This applies to everyone except Road Warriors, who are in the air or behind the wheel for great stretches of time. For them the rules are different: The road is their office, and they just put on their happy face and drive.

For the rest of you, here are a few tips:

How long do you stay? Let's say you're going to New Orleans and want to stay an extra three days for Mardi Gras. The duration of your trip depends on how well situated you are in your company. If you've been paying your dues, you can afford to make the call in your favor—but you have to be sure that you're held in high esteem. Otherwise, skip the festivities.

Do you take the kids? You can now and then, but don't talk about it unless your company prides itself on the good press it gets for being family-friendly.

Do you charge the company for everything you buy? Only if you want a reputation as a cheapskate. Don't submit a voucher for every shoe shine and every newspaper. There are always going to be borderline calls, and nickeling-and-diming—particularly if you've been someplace nice—looks bad (see Nothing but the Truth). Word gets around the office, and soon you become known as the guy who tried to expense-account a gumball.

Are boondoggles advisable? Only if you've been at your company forever or you're Very Senior. Even then you can't take them too often. And as you go trotting off to the Bahamas for that charity golf tournament, you should always make it clear that your trip is going to yield some kind of potential gain for the company.

Are suntans acceptable? Not if you're coming back to a northern winter. Slather on that SPF 50 before your afternoon meeting on the fishing boat. The kind of person who flaunts a tan is only skin-deep.

Who do you hang out with? People from the same company hang together as distinctly as cliques in a high school cafeteria. But keep in mind: Trips don't democratize the workplace. Even if two dozen of you are off on the road together, that doesn't mean that the lowest associates and the senior vice presidents will spend downtime together. If you're a low-level guy, and a bunch of top executives are going out for dinner, don't join them unless, for some reason, they insist. Otherwise you stifle their conversation: Not only can't they complain about how hard it is to get good help these days, they can't complain about you. (If, on the other hand, it's a bunch of lower levels and one vice president going out for a bite, Ms. VP can go, but if she's smart she'll leave early so that the others can complain about how hard it is to find a good job, and about her.)

How much do you take with you? As much as you need—but never walk through the office loaded down with suitcases, particularly if you want to move up the food chain: **It's a status violation to look like a pack animal.**

Still a few more tips on air travel:

Don't travel in a higher class than your boss. If he's not going first-class, you're not, either—even if you can do it with frequent flyer miles. Nor should you sit on an aisle when he's stuck in a middle seat. At the gate, you should ask the attendant for Mr. So-and-So's seat, and make sure it's better than yours. Also, if you belong to a frequent-flyer club, and he doesn't, don't leave him by the gate while you're lounging with a drink.

And don't cheat on your frequent flyer miles. Nearly every company has rules. The people in your company who track these things aren't dumb, and when they find out that you've been storing your miles in your personal account, you'll have no plausible excuse outside of stupidity, which, if you think about it for a moment, you don't want to be considered a plausible excuse.

Hide your phobias. It's perfectly normal to be afraid of flying, but don't advertise it. If you can stomach the trip, then do so without complaining. Most of all, if you're going with a group, don't load yourself up with tranquilizers or alcohol. There you are, squeezed next to your arch-rival in coach, and you're so self-medicated that you're confiding in him your obsession with the boss's spouse, and by the way, is there an airbag handy?

A Special Tip for travel mates: If you've got a spouse or lover traveling along, Spouse must keep in mind that this is work. The job of a spouse or lover is to converse pleasantly, to make everyone else comfortable, and to not submarine your career. Travel mates aren't supposed to have fun. Fun is for vacations. One of the most common political mistakes people make is not briefing their traveling companions on appropriate behavior. The next thing you know, you're back in the office and everyone's still talking about your spouse's half-naked lambada with the hotel's sexy dance instructor.

━◈ The Evil Twin on travel: Other people's travel offers fertile time and space for the Evil Twin. In fact, when someone's away it's so easy to play, "I tried to reach you, but . . ." that it's not recommended behavior.

One strategy that does work is to take advantage of traveler's anxiety. Everyone is crazed a few days before taking off on long trips. There's no way to accomplish all the tasks that must be completed before leaving. What better time for the Evil Twin to wave a memo under someone's nose and ask, "What do you think?" in order to get a "Fine" in response to a request that would normally be denied.

Another Evil Twin option, and one that's often been used on me, is to wait until the traveler returns, particularly when the trip involved crossing many time zones. Immediately accost your target with important matters, and this time you get a kind of dizzy response that you can subsequently mold into whatever you need, since the time-baffled object of your evil probably won't remember what she said. At least, I never did. I still don't.

Tip: If the trip was a particularly nice one, your subordinates and less well-positioned peers will be jealous that you were the one who got to go, and at least one of them will have unleashed his or her Evil Twin while you were gone. Your job upon your return is to figure out within forty-eight hours who it was and to launch the appropriate damage control.

PRIVATE PARTS

It's a gal thing. Now that I'm a consultant and my time is my own, I've been training myself to drink lots of water during the day. I'd spent the last ten years making myself do the opposite—go without water for long periods of time. Why? I was often the only woman at meetings, and I decided not to constantly excuse myself to make trips to the bathroom. Women go more often than men. It's a fact. But I was damned if I was going to let this interrupt my meetings or my career. So, like many other women surrounded by large-bladdered men, I learned to hold it.

It's a guy thing: The first time Gene went to the men's room at his new job, he stood at the urinal and was barely unzipping when the company's CEO marched up to the other urinal. Gene froze. He just stood there, unable to do a thing, turning red, while the CEO relieved himself at great length. It wasn't until the CEO left the room that Gene could get anything to flow.

There's no getting around the fact that we're all mammals, and our biological needs don't stop just because we're wearing designer clothes and using expensive technology. We still have to go to the bathroom, which means that the toilet is part of the political landscape.

The bathroom is the one place at work in which, unless equal opportunity goes further than anyone could currently imagine, men and women are segregated. And that means it's a bonding place for same-sex friendships.

I've actually hired employees in the ladies' room. Once I was looking for a division manager and mentioned my plight to a peer, Wilma. I thought I was simply asking her for help but, while reapplying her lipstick, Wilma asked for the job. I gave it to her, and from then on we called the bathroom our office, since that's where we did most of our serious talking—but only after we checked out the stalls to make sure they were empty.

To succeed in politics it's important to have good bathroom patter at your disposal. Postmeeting tea leaf–sifting takes place there, as does interpretation of other office events. And the way people talk to each other in the bathroom intimates as much as clothes or language.

My friend Barney knew he was in trouble during a downsizing period at the office when the CEO, who was formerly supportive, stopped chatting with him at the urinal. Sure enough, Barney lasted only a few more months.

Bear in mind: **People notice bathroom habits.** I remember one guy who seemed to go to the bathroom every half hour. No one said anything for a year until a secretary piped up: "Have you ever seen anyone with smaller tanks than Joey?" From that moment on Joey was known throughout the office as Tiny Tanks.

Comfort level drops below zero when, as children and euphemistic adults say, it's time for number two. Military guys tend to be the only ones at ease chatting stall to stall. They grew up learning to do this. The rest of us are allowed to be very private. In fact, most men will pick the stall farthest away from others; one friend of mine can't understand why any architect would place three stalls in a bathroom, since no one uses the middle one.

How you announce to others that you want to go to the bathroom is a barometer of intimacy. Euphemisms change as people become friendlier—from the meaningless "Excuse me" down to "I have to take a leak." Or comfort is shown when people start using their favorite phrases—such as when a close male friend tells me "I've got to go to the sandbox." If you're not sure what to say, you can always stick with the neutral "I have to hit the head." But don't get cute. I knew a woman who used to say "It's tinkle time." She was middle management for life.

For certain men, the announcement is made simply by striding down the hall with a *Wall Street Journal* folded beneath one arm. This tends to drive women crazy, since it's only men, and usually only powerful men, who do this.

Away from the office, at conferences and meetings, the euphemisms run wild, from, "It's time for housekeeping notes" to "Everyone can go stretch now." Or, if they're really with it: "Let's take a biology break."

Which brings up the home office, too. A while back a friend was working on resolving a difficult security situation: An employee suffering a nervous breakdown had brought a knife to the office and was threatening to kill his manager. He then left my friend's office, ostensibly to track down his prey. My friend was at a loss what to do, so he made a few calls until he found an expert who made his living counseling people on how to work through such situations. The man had a deep, reassuring voice, and his advice was sound, but my friend detected a strange pattern to his breathing. Then, before he reached the end of the conversation, he heard the toilet flush. He hadn't known the doctor was working from home.

Just because you work at home doesn't mean you're alone. The moment you're on the phone, you're connected to the world. Show some dignity.

Special mention: Many companies now have gyms, or offer gym memberships, which means that you may well find yourself working out or toweling down next to your boss or your assistant. After you've seen someone nude, he or she will never look quite the same. Remember that before you note your colleagues are in the shower and decide to check out what shape they're in.

There are times when you won't be able to avoid naked camaraderie, but gauge how comfortable your superior feels before making a move. If he's awkward, don't prance around. On the other hand, if he's a guy's guy and struts around the locker room without a care in the world, you're the one who's going to seem odd if you're cowering inside the towel bin.

The Evil Twin on private affairs: Whenever an Evil Twin uses the bathroom, things are going to get a little petty. And I don't recommend being petty with Mother Nature. But I have heard of people who have done just that. Sometimes it's worked, and sometimes it hasn't.

For instance: I knew one woman, Judith, who was loathed by her staff for her churlish machinations and her single-minded quest for success. Like many driven people, Judith was well stocked with obsessions, and among them was her need to go to the bathroom alone. One day the women on her staff, fed up with Judith, decided to spell each other in the women's room: There wasn't a moment when one of them wasn't in it, and rather conspicuously so. Whenever Judith thought she could manage a quick trip, she never found herself alone, which meant that by the end of the day the woman was a pain-wracked mess.

Another petty but effective maneuver a friend confided: In most corporations, the CEO, and maybe a few other top people, have their own bathrooms. Sometimes these are open to the plebeians, sometimes not. An Evil Twin I know once steered a new vice president into the room, assuring him this was within protocol, only to have the new kid run into the CEO, who was more proprietary about his bathroom than about his wife.

SMOOTH OPERATOR

Telephone technology is always changing. First there was the phone, a convenient way to talk to one other person. The phone begat the squawk box and the conference call, with which you could talk to a few more people. Then came faxes, and modems, and voice mail, and the Internet, and now the phone is your connection to the world.

For the most part, people get the phone right. It rings, they answer, they talk, they hang up. And they call in cyber-kids to hook them up to whatever they don't understand.

Still, there are a few constantly shifting rules of etiquette to keep in mind. Phone manners fluctuate like fashions. For instance, in the 1980s it was prestigious to have someone place calls for you. In the 1990s, that's considered a sign of corporate waste—unless you're so senior you really don't have the time.

Likewise, the person who answers your phone is also subject to the ups and downs of the status stock market. Answering your own phone is the mark of an executive who's down-to-earth, but there are times that require screening, and then the voice answering your phone matters. Assistants with expensive accents, especially English, are a status symbol. Many female executives like having young men answer their phones, but that's another already waning fad.

There's also etiquette regarding how you handle your voice mail. For instance, some people like to change their messages every day, all day. "Hi, it's Blair at noon on the twenty-first, and I'll be out of the office until three-fifteen." That's good unless it's already the twenty-fifth, and then Blair sounds lost. Also, you don't want to get too cute: "Hey there! You've reached Blair! I'll call you back fast as a hare!" Boss calls, boss hears message, boss hangs up.

Some people like to have their voice mail answered by someone else, which allows them to be spoken of in the third person. "Blair isn't in now, but you can leave a message for him . . ." While acceptable, this is also somewhat pretentious. And the moment it becomes truly pretentious, Blair better change that message or he's going to be losing points every time the machine clicks on.

Because phone manners change constantly, the bottom line is: **Use your phone as a practical tool and not as a status symbol.** Not only will you get more work done, you won't have to worry as much about whether you're getting the phone thing right.

Message slip triage: The order in which people return phone calls is based on utility. Everyone has a heap of messages, usually arranged in terms of each call's importance. Therefore there's a constant relationship between where you are in someone else's stack and how well you're doing. If nobody's returning your phone calls quickly, you know you're in trouble.

Another way to tell you're down is when people learn your voice mail system well enough to use it as an avoidance tool. For instance, you're never at the office after 5 P.M. on Wednesdays, and people are always leaving you messages on Wednesday at five-fifteen. They don't really want to talk to you, but they don't want to snub you, either.

Caution: Voice mail is becoming very sophisticated. A good system allows people to attach copies, or distribute copies through the building, or make blind copies, or more. The same rules for memos apply to phone messages: Just as you don't write down what you don't want anyone other than the addressee to see, don't say what you don't want other people to hear. You call a peer and say, "I've decided I can't deal with Ashley anymore." Maybe your peer's angry at you. Maybe his Evil Twin is running. It's very easy for him to forward count, they heard the sudden *click, click, click* of the pen. They knew that meant their boss didn't like something in their pitch, but they didn't know what. They fell apart. They couldn't hear themselves talk anymore. All they could hear was the pen clicking until the clock ran out—and they did, too.

The audio equivalent of the calm and composed visual appearance is the nonresponse response. Whenever you get a new piece of information that you don't quite understand or like, respond with caution. Don't give away your feelings before you can think them through. **The perfection of the nonresponse is an office necessity.**

Over the years I've adopted the completely uninterpretable, but indispensable, "Huh." Someone can tell me that there's a fly on the computer or that the building's on fire, and if I'm not sure what the real story is, I'll say "Huh" in such a way as to indicate nothing.

Everyone I've ever met in a power position had such a phrase, including "I hear you," "That's an idea," "Interesting," or the ever-popular "Really," said without any inflection whatsoever. "Really" can also be used when you disagree with a statement or opinion but don't want to go on record having done so. Opinionated statement: "I think the Aggies are the best college football team in America." Measured reply: "Really."

Work on your non-response response. Practice saying it until you're sure that it gives away nothing, then use it as a space bar to buy yourself time and room.

Tip: **In a crisis, look your best.** Too often people trapped in mass hysteria take on the appearance of the crisis personified: bad hair, stained ties, torn hose. Wrong. Don't look like you're a mess just because you're caught in one.

A constant, composed demeanor can even boost morale in trying times. During a period when Prudential Securities was under fire, I dressed as nicely as possible, since nervous types were looking at me for indications of the company's health, desperate for cues . So every morning I spent significant time getting it together. The message was: Things must be okay or Ronna would be looking worse.

Many people believe that they should look as though they're working around the clock, particularly when they are. "Aren't you impressed with my incredible suffering?" they're saying. My experience is that, when everyone's working hard, it's often those who look worst who are contributing the least; they're more concerned with showing off their war wounds than with doing their share.

The Crying Game: Sometimes people do lose their game faces. At its worst, that means tears. For the most part, crying is never okay at the office, unless there's a major tragedy, in which case you can cry discreetly (and I mean *very* discreetly—my cousin once lost a relative and was tearing up in his office; his assistant was so unsettled by the sight that she strode over to his door and slammed it shut).

The worst tears of all are those of frustration, which indicate that not only can't you handle the load, you can't handle your emotions. The best tears are the ones you manage to just hold back—when a man does this, he looks sensitive; when a woman does it, she looks tough. Either way is a win.

When men can cry: when they drink too much and start sounding like beer commercials ("I love you guys"). That's considered macho, and it's okay as long as it happens outside the office.

—⟳ The Evil Twin on a constant demeanor: The Evil Twin is always scoping out others. So when an adversary shows up looking worse than usual, the Evil Twin notices it immediately and makes sure that everyone else does, too—but taking care to make the announcement while astride the proverbial high horse.

For instance, your sworn enemy Harvey has been nipping at your heels for years. Whenever you've been down, Harve's been the first to pounce on you. Now Harve's going through a bad time him-

those words over to Ashley with a little comment ("Thought you ought to hear this"). Now you and Ashley are enemies for life.

More caution: Beware the squawk box. I once was on a conference call at a time when I was home sick and so medicated that I forgot a few rules, and off I went on a tirade against a co-worker. The co-worker, of course, was sitting in the office, listening. Remember: Anyone can hit that button at will. One Hollywood executive, famous for reaming out her assistants, was flaming one of them for some tiny mistake when the assistant broke. She silently summoned her colleagues to her phone, whereupon she turned on the box and treated her office to her boss's tirade.

(Hollywood's rules for phone calls are so different from those of every other industry that a neophyte won't be able to make any sense of them. If for some reason you find yourself having to deal with the movie business, the bottom line is: There are no rules. Anything can and does happen on the phone. For instance, it's not uncommon to receive a phone call from an executive's assistant, asking if you're in for Ms. Important. "I am," you say, thinking this means she's calling you. Maybe, maybe not. "Please hold," says the assistant. Perhaps ten minutes later you realize that the assistant was ordered to place several calls at once, and Ms. Important is talking to whomever she was able to reach in her own preferred order. You may or may not ever actually talk to her.)

Still more caution: Beware personal calls. Everyone makes them, so that in itself is not a problem. But don't drag emotional issues into the office through the phone lines. One gay woman with whom I worked many years ago was completely in the closet—she thought. The problem was that she used to fight with her lover in a voice that should have been saved for home. The rest of us had to pretend we didn't know she was gay, yet not only did we know it, we knew more intimate details of her roller-coaster relationship than her close friends did.

Still one more caution: Be smart about calls from cars, airplanes, and street corners. Sometimes they're necessary, and in some industries they're acceptable and even routine. But in many others they're not; the quality of such calls is often bad and the effect can be pretentious. Maybe you're calling from a car phone only because you're rushed, but to the recipient that call can mean "You're not important enough for me to call you from the office."

⮜ The Evil Twin on the telephone: First, you must institute excellent systems for returning calls. For some, that means each call must be returned by the end of the day; for others, within forty-eight hours. More important than an exact time is an exact method: For instance, establish a routine that puts your habitual callers at ease when they don't hear from you the next day; you're clearly someone who takes two days to return the call—but return it you do and must.

Once these patterns are fixed, your Evil Twin can thrive. If everyone knows your routine, you can make one, and only one, person crazy by not adhering to it. When he complains to others, they'll look startled: "But Chip always returns his calls within two days." Your antagonist now knows something's up, but he doesn't know quite enough to do anything about it.

Playing with phone habits can be a mind game that I don't advise you to use except with the most pernicious people. When they leave a message begging you to call them before their deadline at five, you call at five-ten with a satisfactory excuse in hand. Or you call them at the exact moment you know they're not at their desk. But sinking any further is wrongheaded.

At one office, where everyone's voice mail has a three-digit personal code, one woman who was furious at a co-worker spent weeks figuring out her code, and then called randomly during the week to erase important messages. That was not Evil Twin. That was Downright Mean and Nasty.

VIRTUAL POLITICS

Branch offices have their own politics, which allows you to avoid a great deal of what makes the home office so difficult: No one sees much of you, and since they don't see you, they often forget to involve you. The downside is that you're never at the head of the line for handouts. Let's say I'm the Big Boss and I have a limited bonus pool. It's down to a bigger increase for Amy, who sits right outside my door, or Meg, who's based in Tokyo. I may like Meg a great deal more than Amy, and even suspect that Meg's more talented. But Amy's a pain, so I'll probably give her more than Meg. It may not even be conscious. But at some level, I know I'll have Amy in my face, whereas with Meg the worst possibility is having her in my ear.

Technology, however, is changing all this. Virtual politics means that everyone can be right here. Or that everyone can be equally distant from the center. The virtual workplace is more fluid, with more players. More people can position themselves for attention, at any time, without walking into the Boss's office. They can send E-mail or V-mail, and they can send it from almost anywhere in the world, and they can send it anytime they want.

The old vertical model that molded modern bureaucracy—directives come down, information goes up—is becoming obsolete. Now you can move horizontally and diagonally. You can jump, you can rise, you can fall. Someone once told me the rules for survival when driving in Rome: Assume that any vehicle can and will go in any direction at any time. It's pretty much the same with information today.

In other words, **the virtual world has redefined the geography of office politics.** You could have just presented what you believe to be the best report of your life, and then, without warning, some pixel monkey in Lubbock points out potentially crippling flaws in your assumptions—some guy who otherwise would never have been able to get anywhere near you or your group, some guy who's now positioning his team to take over from yours with just a few taps on the computer keyboard.

It's too soon to say exactly what virtual politics will do to office politics, but there are hints. Technology has already intensified the political game by expanding the number of players and the number of hours available—and, at the same time, introducing more possibilities of random or unexpected acts. Things go places they shouldn't have gone. Good office politics has always been similar to chess. When you add virtual politics, it's like a chess game that's abruptly expanded into 3-D. In other words, these days we're all pioneers in a new dimension, boldly going where none of us has gone before.

Tip: **Virtual sex is more than virtually dangerous.** Unlike a letter, which you can rewrite until it's just right, or a phone message, in which you hear your own words spoken aloud, on-line communication is a different story. You're sitting alone, it's fast and it's easy, you're typing quickly, the other person's typing quickly, you send out an E-mail that's slightly flirtatious, you get back something that's more so, and it builds. It's easy to mistake the immediacy of electronic communications for intimacy, especially late at night or early in the morning, when you're just checking in because you're on the road and you can't sleep. It takes only a few E-mail notes before you think you're involved in something much more intimate than anything happening in real life. You're wrong.

A recent case from Silicon Valley: When Lisa met Bart it was very late at night and they were on opposite ends of California. Still, their E-mail took them places neither had ever been before, and soon they fell in love. They worked in the same field, had similar

backgrounds, and were equally excited about digital commerce—so much so, in fact, that when Bart had an opening in his department he offered it to Lisa, who moved from San Diego up to Sunnyvale to take the job.

They then commenced their affair in real life, but things didn't go as well. Bart still loved Lisa, but Lisa decided that she preferred the Bart who sent compellingly passionate messages at 3 A.M.to the Bart who bossed her around at work. Bart noticed Lisa's coolness and began to pester and provoke her, demanding they spend more time together. Lisa responded with a sexual harassment suit, and as backup, she printed out every love note that Bart had ever sent her on-line. Unlike Bart, she'd been saving anything and everything. Upshot: Bart lost his job. The moral: **Don't leave an E-mail trail.**

It's not just about sex. By now everyone's heard a story involving incriminating E-mail sent to the wrong person. And every year companies send out messages warning users that no E-mail is ever truly private and that the company may store all of them somewhere in the giant mainframe in the sky. But everyone forgets this.

⚓ The Evil Twin on cyberspace: Here's an early '80s story from a media concern that had just moved to a primitive form of E-mail called messaging, which allowed employees to send notes on their computers that couldn't be saved or printed.

A senior management spot had just opened up, and Cal, a bright young Native American, approached one of the company's three top bosses and asked to be considered. The man thanked Cal for his interest, insisted that he would keep him in mind, and sent him back to his desk.

There, a few minutes later, Cal accidentally received a message intended for the two other Top Guns. It said, basically, that this bozo thought he was good enough to make it into the inner circle, but that he wasn't "our kind." Cal immediately understood what had happened, and let his Evil Twin take over.

Once Cal turned off his computer, the note would be gone for good, so he ran off and found the one computer wonk who, he guessed, would be sympathetic. "Are there any circumstances under which a message can be printed and saved?" he asked. He then brought the woman to his computer, showed her the message, and she found a way to make a copy.

Cal went back to the man who'd sent the message and presented him with the hard copy. "I just thought you'd want to see this," he said, smiled, and left without saying another word. A week later, his promotion was announced.

YOU ARE WHERE YOU EAT

When Zach, the president of a publishing company, started his job, the Powers That Be advised him to find a nearby restaurant unfrequented by others at the company so he could wine and dine without being overheard. Zach searched around until he settled on a grotto-like café where he felt safe speaking in a normal tone of voice, and over the next few years he used the place often, mostly to fire people—although he was oblivious to just how often he'd done that.

One day, taking an assistant out to a friendly lunch, Zach started ambling toward the café. But the moment the assistant saw where they were heading, she burst into tears and screamed, "How could you?" She then fled down the block, leaving Zach completely mystified until, back at the office, another assistant explained to him the restaurant's negative connotation.

Everyone has to eat, so food is an integral part of every job. In fact, in some industries you'll get more done while sitting on a banquette than behind a desk. As a result, everything concerning food—specific restaurants, types of foods, snacks in the afternoon—takes on a far greater significance than if it were eaten and consumed in private.

There are basically four business meals: breakfast, lunch, dinner, and drinks (and, for some, coffee). Each meal has a different meaning and a different purpose, and it varies from industry to industry, as well as from region to region.

For the most part, breakfast is best shared with those you gen-

uinely want to see. It's a more intimate setting than lunch—people tend to be less guarded, their shells haven't quite hardened, there's still a little sleep left in their eyes. Projects are much more likely to start over breakfast than to close.

Lunch is seldom as casual as breakfast—or as formal as dinner. It is, in essence, the major meal of the office. Therefore it's colored by certain expectations, because industry rituals always come into play, whether it's the choice of restaurant, the food, or the time. Noon can be exactly right or unforgivably early; one-thirty chic or unacceptably late. A sandwich can lend the exact informal touch, or be exactly wrong.

The people you choose to invite for lunch from outside your office depend on your job and your needs, and you're the only one who can decide. Whom you invite from inside the office is a thornier question. Asking someone senior to lunch can feel awkward, but you should do it now and then. Phrase it in such a way that Senior Person can decline without embarrassment: For example, ask on the spur of the moment, particularly if you know Senior Person is free that day. This way she can decline without feeling she's put you down. If you beg for a date anytime at all in the future, you're putting her on the spot, and you'll probably wind up with a last-minute cancellation.

Most interoffice lunches are with peers, whom you can invite according to your office rules (some offices encourage interoffice lunch, many discourage it). **If you always eat with people junior to you, it communicates a message, as does only eating with people senior to you.**

Subordinates love to be invited to lunch, but be careful not to ask the same ones over and over, or others will start wondering why. And assume that they'll hit on you for something while you're eating together, since they've got you trapped.

Where you eat depends on how comfortable you are with your

companions, whether you're trying just to please them, and how defended you want to be. The good ol' guys at most companies eat lunch every day at the same place—they're the ones who announce how it's done: "We go to Patsy's, we go at noon, and we eat steak." If you're new to the office, it's a compliment when you're asked. But remember that if you start eating lunch every day with the People Who Always Eat Together, extricating yourself from that crowd can cause hard feelings.

Some people eat at the same restaurant so often that it serves as their office nickname. My favorite was a man nicknamed "42" because every single day he ate lunch *and* dinner at Manhattan's 21 Club.

Lunch at your desk is corporate-culture dependent. So is skipping lunch, which used to be the mark of a macho Wall Streeter. At some places not noticing lunch is a badge of hardworking honor ("Wow—is it four-thirty already?"). At others, it means you're too unpopular to find a lunch date. Same with the corporate cafeteria: Some CEOs won't eat anywhere else, to prove that they're down to earth—or that they're cheap. Others would find it embarrassing to be caught eating next to the maintenance people.

Dinner is more quirky. For one, it depends if it's in town or out of town, where the rules are different. At a conference or a business trip, a dinner can be a chance to unwind in a strange place or to forge better relationships. At home, dinners tend to be more about relationships than lunch since, being longer, there's more capacity for intimacy—and you're more likely to drink at night, which can mean loose talk.

Dinner takes people away from their families, so it's not always appropriate. Dinners are best used when recruiting; as in a courtship, you can seldom impress with a quick lunch. A fancy dinner is more memorable. And the more you want them, the fancier the dinner.

Some people like tea. Most people don't. Tea has a somewhat

feminine connotation, so if you're a woman, save tea for your girl-friends; if you're a man, have tea only when you see an advantage in demonstrating you're a sensitive guy.

Drinks are for when you do want to see someone but you don't have a lot of time. It's the coffee date of business. The hidden message is, "I'd like to get together, but then I have to be somewhere more important."

A word on snacking at the office: The food you choose can type-cast you forever. One friend became known throughout her office as Muffin Momma because she brought a muffin in to work every morning and then kept it on her desk all day, nibbling at the crumbs. Likewise, Pizza Mouth was a good-looking, clear-complexioned lawyer who ate pizzas at his desk whenever he could, often leaving small traces of them on his lower lip. At an Arizona newspaper, one woman was dubbed the Squirrel for her tendency to bring food into the office, hide it so she wouldn't eat it all at once, and then forget; people would discover chocolate bars in her in-box and vegetable dip on her copy. After she left, her assistant went through her desk drawers and found an ancient plate of scrambled eggs.

Tip: People use food in the office as a form of bonding. For instance, if your boss is fond of chocolate, more likely than not you will see several of your associates carrying fancy one-pound boxes into her office. The hope is that the boss will be overwhelmed with her need to indulge and then invite the donor to stay, whereupon she'll shut the door and the two of them can bond. As a rule, high-fat and other comfort foods tend to be consumed in private, which make them ideal for secret sharing.

Tip: Timing at meals is important. Unless you're dealing with someone with whom you're completely comfortable, if you've got something important to discuss, don't bring it up when you sit down. Not only is it bad manners to rush into your business, you run the risk

of getting a negative answer from your dining partner and then having to sit through two more courses with nothing else to say.

—⟨ The Evil Twin on eating on the job: Food supplies the Evil Twin with hundreds of opportunities. For instance, you can use your restaurant habits to throw people off balance. If you normally eat at an expensive gourmet restaurant, take a disliked employee to a diner and he'll get the hint. Or use meals to ply information, knowing the habits of your targets. Force an evening person to come to a 7 a.m. breakfast, take someone whose mouth is loosened by liquor out to drinks. (But never try to make a recovering alcoholic drink. That's beyond evil.)

You can also use food within the office for your own benefit. One of my favorite examples is from an executive recruiting firm where my friend had an unpleasant employee, Ted, who for political reasons could not be fired. Whenever Ted was ready to present an idea, my friend launched Death by Food: She'd schedule a meeting to discuss the idea at 1 P.M., and insist that all present first indulge in the heavy luncheon food she provided. By the time Ted started to speak, everyone else was starting to snore.

I Will Survive

(How to Manage Your Attitude, Your Head,
Your Reputation, Your Looks . . .)

CLOTHES CALLS

COME BLOW YOUR OWN HORN

I'D RATHER BE RED THAN DEAD

NICE GUYS FINISH LAST

PUT ON A HAPPY FACE

SIZE MATTERS

SPEAKING IN TONGUES

YOU'RE NOT IN THE ARMY NOW

CLOTHES CALLS

I'll say it straight out. **The problem with clothes is that they say all the things you're trying not to say with your mouth.**

What are these things? How about: "I'm not sure who I am." "I can't decide what I want." "I don't think I'm executive caliber." "I think I'm better than you." "I don't think I'm better than you." "I want to be like you." "I'm not like you at all."

Your attire tells others what you think of yourself and what you think of them. Clothes are one of the best manifestations of self-opinion around. An intelligent grasp of clothes shows you have complete and total possession of your person. It sends a message that you know who you are and you know who your peers are, as well as your bosses. You don't stand out (unless you need to), and you don't disappear into the scenery (unless you choose to).

The ultimate rule for wardrobe selection: **Dress for the corporate culture.** Clothes aren't about taste unless you're in a business where taste matters. If you're working at a company where everyone's wearing blue polyester leisure suits, and you want to advance in the company, you'd better start shopping for blue polyester, too.

For instance, at many places men are supposed to wear a coat and tie to work, but the moment they get to the office, they take the jacket off, hang it on the back of the door, and don't put it on again until they leave. (If they do wear the jacket during the day, peo-

ple assume they're going either to a funeral or to a job interview.) It doesn't matter that this makes no sense. Follow the leader.

Another example: Sean, a newly hired editor at a national publication, came to his first editorial meeting at the magazine owner's private mansion dressed in a suit and tie. He was shocked to see his boss had on jeans and a T-shirt, while the publisher showed up in tennis shorts. Sean couldn't figure out what was going on until the magazine's owner appeared, wearing black silk pajamas. Sean didn't switch to PJs at his next meeting, but he did ditch the suit.

The penultimate rule: **Dress for your rung on the ladder.** If you're a messenger, don't wear a three-piece suit. If you're a vice president, don't wear jeans (unless the president does). Unfortunately, people's judgment can get clouded, especially during times of change (see Politics in the Time of Cholera). For instance, when a hip Silicon Valley company was bought by a more conservative southeastern outfit, clothes anxiety overcame the company and compromises took place throughout all levels. For months no one could tell who was who: The new owners, trying to look cool, wore jeans (but pressed ones, which didn't work), and the low-level suck-ups from the tech company started wearing ties (but tasteless ones, which also didn't work). It wasn't until the company settled down that everyone's clothing habits returned to normal.

But let's say you get the basics right. Beware: It's the accessories that do in most people.

For men, watches, shoes, and ties say it all.

Watches are basically sports cars on men's wrists. Guys look at each other's watches. They can't help it. In brief, watches range from those that say, "I'm extremely rich and I want you to know it," to "I'm too cool to care about money." You can find both kinds on CEOs—the guy who waves his diamond-studded watch three inches from your eyes, or the guy with a black plastic Swatch designed to make the little people think he's one of them.

Also: If he got his money from his family, he usually wears an expensive but understated Swiss watch. If he's an Ivy Leaguer (or wants you to think he is), he sports a leather band, often worn. If he's trendy, he wears something so hip it's hardly identifiable as a time-piece. If he's screaming for attention, he goes for something odd, like a Mickey Mouse watch. And then there are those calculator watches, on which no one does any calculations. They're there to say, "I'm different."

Shoes tell another story. Ivy League types change their watch-bands to match their shoes—brown with brown, black with black. A downtown banker wears lace-up shoes, plain toe or wing tip. He'd probably get fired if he didn't. Loafers with tassels mean you don't work on Wall Street. Spit and polish matter if you're older than Generation X. Guys who've been in the service have shinier shoes than those who haven't. Bill Clinton is a perfect example: Whatever else senior executives may think of him, the former soldiers among them find his constantly unshined shoes a disgrace.

Ties are another major male announcement. Do you want to be noticed or ignored? Next time you see Donald Trump on television, study his tie—if you can do it without sunglasses. He wants to be noticed. On the other hand, a couple of years ago, I attended a Major Business Luncheon in Washington. This was long before Dolly, the Scottish sheep, was cloned, so I couldn't have been looking at two hundred copies of the same guy. But it seemed that way, since all the men in the room wore virtually identical ties.

Final note on male accessories: **Don't be the only peacock in a cage of pigeons.** Take the case of Derek, who was too pretty—but it wasn't just about looks. Although men can have a difficult time with other males' attractiveness, the right attitude can prove you're one of the guys. It was the finishing touches that doomed Derek. The other men couldn't deal with the pocket handkerchief, the alligator shoes, the perfectly capped teeth, the year-round tan.

Too much money and too many accessories were going into keeping Derek pretty. What the effort said was "It's important to me that I look better than all of you." (The other guys used to say that Derek looked as if he'd just stepped out of a men's fashion magazine. This wasn't meant as a compliment.)

Inverse Rule: **Don't be the only pigeon in a cage of peacocks.** If every man in your company wears pinky rings, gold necklaces, and white shoes, then you'd better consider making some new purchases.

With women, the hair and the nails are key.

A woman's hairstyle itself isn't as important as how it compares to those of her peers. In certain parts of the country you want your hair to be blond, immobile, and to extend as far from your skull as possible. Elsewhere, close-cropped brunettes are in fashion, and so is gray hair, if it's striking.

More important to notice than hair itself, which most women eventually get right, are hairstyle shifts. A change in a woman's hair, color or cut, can signify a change in ambition. For instance, sometimes you'll see a women fluff out: She'll wear more feminine clothes and her hair will get softer. Fluffing out usually means she's focusing on something other than the job, most likely in her personal life.

Color is also important. By the time most women on the rise hit forty-five, they're coloring their hair; and if they want to look pulled together, those roots can't show. That means going in every month for processing, and that's a significant chunk of time, as well as cash, to invest. So what this routine really says is, "I have enough money and enough control over my schedule to take care of my hair on a regular basis."

Likewise, as for the red or gold highlights you see in women's hair: God didn't make those. Paulo or Mr. Jon did. Women pay a lot of money for those strands of color. They say, "Pay attention to me. I'm willing to spend even more money so that you'll know I'm a heavy hitter."

Just as men look at other men's watches, women look at each other's nails. Executives don't paint cute designs on their nails. Nor do they wear nail jewelry. If you want to be taken seriously, your nails must look like every other corporate woman's nails. To achieve that, you have a standing appointment with Gracel or Marta once a week. It's that message again: "I'm in control of myself and my time."

Keep in mind: **Once you're truly important, you're allowed one dress violation.** As in music or art, where you have to master the form before you can violate it, you must understand clothes well before you can digress well, whether it's via red socks, a polka-dot bow tie, or a singular piece of jewelry. Clothing eccentricity signals power. You've gone beyond the couplet. You've mastered the epic poem, and now you're writing free verse. You're reinventing some classic idea of form in a way that makes everyone understand you have more confidence than they do.

A Tip on Casual Day: Casual Day basically means that employees have yet another worry: What does *casual* mean? Are jeans too informal? (Sometimes.) Is a sports coat too formal? (Sometimes.) Some say Casual Day allows employees to save money on clothes, but few people do, because what's casual at the workplace isn't casual at home, so everyone has to go out and buy a third wardrobe of casual-but-still-presentable clothes for the office. The drill is the same as on other days. Look around. What does the most popular guy in the office wear? What do the boss's favorites have on? What does the least-liked person wear? Triangulate these positions and you'll get the right answer.

Special tip on plastic surgery: If you decide that you're going to change your image through a new nose rather than new clothes, expect people to notice. When someone says, "You look different" after you've gotten whatever new feature you've wanted, "I'm parting my hair on the other side" doesn't cut it. People will talk. Get used to it. The worst response to inquiries about liposuction I ever heard was that of a woman who became so fed up with the attention that she

172 WORK WOULD BE GREAT

started informing people that various parts of their body needed work, too. Bad move.

—⊄ The Evil Twin on clothes: You see Enemy (or Enemy's date) at a formal company dinner wearing a rubberized latex bustier, which is squeezing her out of the top like the last bit of toothpaste. "Bambi!" you cry. "You look terrific. You're the only one with enough guts to wear something that livens this place up."

COME BLOW YOUR OWN HORN

Self-promotion is a delicate art that requires much forethought—it's difficult to handle precisely and is therefore easy to bungle. Bad self-promotion makes you look even worse than before you started. Good self-promotion makes you look better. It's that simple. Here are some pointers:

Never steal other people's ideas. It makes them angry; it makes you look stupid. It also convinces others that you don't have much on the ball, if one single idea is so important to you that you'll do anything to own it.

If someone's trying to grab one of your ideas, it's often better to surrender graciously than to engage in a messy fight. Chances are the thief lacks the imagination to know what to do with the idea now that he's got it. Meanwhile, you achieve bonus self-promotion points by avoiding a sloppy, time-consuming mess—provided you make sure your boss knows you chose the high road.

Never put yourself in the spotlight when you know your boss is ready to take a bow herself. Some bosses may be shy, but for the most part, they'd prefer it if they, rather than you, receive the attention. Take the case of ribbon cutting. When I was at Prudential, I was occasionally asked to make a speech or cut a ribbon for a new charity or a foundation. I enjoyed these ceremonies, but nonetheless whenever an invitation turned up for a truly major event that I suspected my boss would like, I'd present it to him. "Hey, Boss," I'd say, "we were invited to speak at the Totally Prestigious School. Should we

accept on your behalf?" It wasn't much of a sacrifice for me, and it always made him feel good.

Delegate self-promotion. Always make sure that one of your allies is fully informed about something you've done. (It never hurts to make a friend out of someone who both talks a lot and is well regarded.) Let him do the work. Your job is to sit quietly with a humble, modest smile while he trumpets your accomplishments. If you can do it with a straight face, occasionally you can even demur.

If you're going to promote yourself as a good person with a good heart, do the good work. If you want to be known as someone who's interested in a charity that's helping to clean up the city, then clean. Everybody knows charity work will improve their image, but some people forget that this works only if you actually do the work. If your idea of generosity is forcing your assistant to paint houses, you're inviting your enemy's Evil Twin to a picnic on your tab.

Tip: Pick an allegiance to an organization that you genuinely care about, as well as one somehow connected to your company's goals (or one that can be connected). For instance, I saw one woman's commitment to breast cancer research earn her telecommunications company a reputation for supporting women and bring her praise for her leadership skills. I watched an African-American man's dedicated work educating minority children help him make the transition to management. And I saw a lawyer's passion for civic infrastructure issues bring him to the attention of an investment banking company's chairman. One of my own biggest career breaks came through someone who noticed my managerial work for the United Way. But you only earn attention when you genuinely care about the issues—and when you put in real time.

Tip: **As far as awards go, it's better to give than to receive.** If you and your outfit can create opportunities that recognize

other people's work, the benefit of being connected to these heroes will rub off on you without the emotional baggage (envy, anger, jealousy) that accompanies winning the award yourself. The light of reflected glory is often more flattering than direct sunlight.

◄ The Evil Twin on self-promotion: If someone's attempts at groundless self-promotion are driving you nuts, the simplest solution is that time-honored technique: point and laugh. Too often this kind of shameless behavior paralyzes other co-workers, who stand around mute, stupefied and amazed that no one will call a spade a spade.

So you do the calling. Here's an example: Recently Charles, one of life's most egregious self-promoters, was filmed participating in a company-sponsored walk-a-thon benefit for cancer patients. This was Mr. Big's pet project, and one to which Charles claimed to have devoted his own heart and soul. Charles was scoring many points until Carrie, a junior-level silent killer, told a few select people that during the event the only time Charles could be seen walking anywhere was when the cameras were on him. This piece of news raced through the office faster than Charles's taxi to the finish line.

I'D RATHER BE RED THAN DEAD

If you're convinced that your idea, and only your idea, is correct, the odds aren't bad that you'll end up dead, in a corporate sense. The biggest insight I gleaned from attending Harvard Business School's Advanced Management Program with 159 peers was that there could be 160 right answers. I don't think I've ever seen any right answer that was completely right over time. But many people think they hold the key, and when they feel that way, they lock themselves into a position from which they can't escape without losing face.

Our times are too complicated for hard-and-fast answers. Remember: **Where you stand shouldn't depend only on where you sit.** Someday you may have to support your opposition's position—careers are fluid, and you can never be sure where your next seat will be.

For instance, let's say you're out in the field and you've been very vocal about your low opinion of the home office. Then one day you get that big promotion, but it means you're now working at the very place you've been railing against. Who's going to believe you when you suddenly swear by the home office? Your allegiance can be accepted only if you held that door open from the beginning.

The failure to compromise is one of the most common non-performance-related reasons people lose jobs. When you paint yourself into a corner, the only thing that can save you is being 100 percent right. And that rarely happens. And even if you are right now, there's still a chance that your inflexibility will bring you grief later.

⟜ The Evil Twin on being absolutely, positively right: When you and a rival are arguing, and he won't budge, step aside and let him win. I've done this several times in the past, and although it can feel completely wrong to allow someone you dislike to win, remember that these sorts of victories are at best temporary. Rival may walk away feeling as though you wimped out. But you didn't. You set Rival up.

For instance: Once an unpleasant office combatant named Gary and I were on opposite sides of how to handle a complicated and expensive project. I saw it one way, Gary the other. The more we fought, the more we backed ourselves into a corner. Then I wised up. The fact was, neither of us knew the right answer.

But I did know that if I gave in, not only would I score diplomacy points with the Big Boss, Gary would be in jeopardy. He'd staked everything on being right, whereas I had nothing to lose: If he was indeed correct, then our team would succeed, and I'd find a way to get a piece of that, as well as look like a team player. If Gary was wrong, he'd go crashing down, because everyone would know that he was the sole motivator behind the effort.

Just in case, my Evil Twin didn't let anyone forget. "Gary's got everything riding on this play," I said. "I just hope he's right." I never stopped referring to the project as Gary's, and when the project did ultimately crater, everyone said, "Did you see what happened to Gary's baby?" His project dead, Gary took months to recover.

NICE GUYS FINISH LAST

Think about the word *nice*. When you do, you'll realize that being nice isn't all that nice. The top people in business may be tough, honest, even humanitarian. But nice? Nice is someone who's not in anyone's way. If, when your name comes up, everyone says, "Oh, what a nice guy," what it usually means is that they'll try not to fire you right before Christmas.

In other words, **Miss Congeniality never becomes Miss America.**

Years ago, when the equivalent of corporate tenure still existed, you could afford to sit in an office for twenty years and be nice. No longer. The business world is littered with stories of the nicest guys in their departments who got fired. Afterward everyone shook their heads and said "What a shame," but in their hearts they weren't surprised. And in some cases their only disappointment stemmed from the fact that the nice guy who'd just got taken out posed no threat. "He's so nice" meant "I could get whatever I wanted from him."

All this doesn't mean you shouldn't have as many other sterling character traits as possible: By all means be moral, thoughtful, decent, reputable, trustworthy, and more. You just don't have to be nice in the process.

⟻ The Evil Twin on being nice: If you're watching someone you know to be smart, aggressive, and ambitious, but all you're seeing is lots of nice, there's a good chance that you're watching an Evil Twin in action.

In parts of the South there's a phrase: "Nicing someone to death." When used as a verb, *nicing* means hiding your intentions by acting sweet. The more intensely Scarlett O'Hara went after her best friend Melanie's husband, the nicer she was to Melanie.

Likewise, when a shark named Roland started wandering into my office, offering me gourmet snacks and grandiose compliments, I knew something was up. Roland was good—he never offered too much. But sharks rarely change stripes, to mix metaphors. After a month of this casual pleasantness, Roland was sitting on my couch munching on an apple out of a fruit basket he'd brought me (pretending all the while that it was an unwanted gift from a client) when he sprang.

"By the way," he said, "I'm starting a new group and I know that Myrna's interested . . ." It turned out that the month of niceness had been preparation for asking if he could pick off one of my senior people.

PUT ON A HAPPY FACE

Question: What should you look like when someone insults you at an important meeting? When the Big Boss dresses you down? When your rival's been promoted? When the phone rings? When the coffee cart rolls past? When the sun sets?

Answer: The same.

Always play with your game face. Cues, positive or negative, help the other side score.

When I was much younger I was often the only woman in my department, and my male co-workers liked to coach me. The comment I received most often: "Boy, would I love to play poker with you!" It wasn't just that my face was giving away my emotions—my entire body was radiating signals. I couldn't bluff.

But a poker face is necessary at the office as well as in cards. If you have employees, they'll be constantly watching you to see if you're happy, unhappy, angry, or distracted, among other things. Your face and body language become their barometer, and the more signals you emit, the more sensitively they'll react, which means they'll put extra time into interpreting you, and that in turn means time away from their own tasks.

If you listen to people talk about their office, you'll hear a great deal about personal signals. Typical story: The chief executive who clicked his pen obsessively whenever he was unhappy. Everyone in the company knew he did this, but no one knew if he was aware of it because no one was brave enough to ask.

At one meeting, while his team was trying to land a new ac-

self—the new Big Guy doesn't cop to his act, and there's been talk that his secretary, with whom he's been having a messy affair, is leaving the state with her new lover. Harve's spiffy suits are starting to look a little worn and a little tired, as is Harve himself. Today he's wearing the same shirt he had on yesterday, with the same fleck of mustard from his hot-dog-in-the-office lunch still stuck to his collar, and his eyes are rimmed with dark circles large enough to pass for target practice.

Wrong Evil Twin move: Make fun of him. Right Evil Twin move: Act sympathetic. "Look at Harvey," you say. "He's looking terrible. I'm so worried about him." The point is to be completely certain that everyone else sees what you see. Now everyone will be scrutinizing Harve for signs of weakness, but all you did was express your deepest, most sincere concern.

SIZE MATTERS

People like to pretend it isn't so. They prefer to think there are more important issues; they dislike its inherent injustice. But your physical dimensions are an important part of your office persona. Like it or not, your body can play as large a part as your ability in others' perceptions of your role.

The first issue: **Height counts.** Tall people have an advantage in the workplace. When someone tall walks into a room, others notice and are more likely to take him or her seriously. People have an unconscious tendency to associate size with power. For example, back in the 1980s a high-profile San Francisco business concern was run by an entrepreneurial father and his oldest son. The father was charismatic and dynamic, the son listless, bland. Often they held staggered meetings; first you met with one, then the other. Afterward, people remembered the father as standing well over six feet, and estimated that the son was a few inches shorter. In reality, the two men were the same height.

Many small men I know harbor a paranoid fantasy that when they're not around big guys make fun of them. This isn't paranoia. Tall guys do make fun of short guys. Every time I had trouble with a short guy at work and I'd talk to a tall guy about it, at some point he'd say, "Well, he's very short," as if that ended it. Tall men and short men have worked out such an intricate routine over the centuries that often the tall man's insults are like dog whistles—they're perceptible only to the short guy's ears.

Being short doesn't mean you can't advance. History is replete with wildly prosperous short men, and psychiatrists have written volumes about how compensating for lack of height can actually propel a man to success. Politically speaking, however, you want to avoid doing the Tiny Tim thing.

Tiny Tim, a successful executive at a company where I once worked, was almost exactly my height, which meant he was five feet, two inches tall. But not everyone knew this, due to Tim's intricate defensive patterns, such as refusing to greet taller people at his door; instead he made them walk into his office and sit down without his leaving his specially designed, elevated chair. Clearly these coping mechanisms made him feel less short, but they also made him an object of ridicule. How do you think he got his nickname?

For women, being short means running the risk of being labeled petite, which makes it hard to be taken seriously. Worse, if you become powerful, you end up being called a Tiny Terror.

Tall is good, big is good, stout is okay—but fat is not. The only way you can win with fat is if you wear it well. Fat people must be better groomed than everyone else to prove that they're not out of control. They're just carrying extra pounds. And if you manage those extra pounds with aplomb, you'll get a minimum of notice. But if the weight starts looking as though it's overwhelming you, if buttons are popping or shirts are ripping, then they'll talk. Loss of sartorial control fascinates people. It signifies loss of emotional control.

Keep in mind: Posture is important. It doesn't matter if you're tall and fit if you don't stand up straight. I once knew a trim, lanky man whose tilting stance eventually earned him a nickname he never shook: Five After Six.

Tip for women: What's the right compliment for a man at the office? You want to say something nice, but you don't want it to sound like a come on. You can't say "Nice butt." You can say, however,

"You've been working out, haven't you?" This implies that the guy looks great without being specific about where he looks great.

The most common mistake women make when trying to flatter a man: commenting on how thin he is. To him, it sounds as though you're saying he's the ninety-eight-pound weakling who gets sand kicked in his face.

Tip for men: Never even hint that a woman's gained weight. When you want to score points, just ask, "You're losing weight, aren't you?" Say that even if she's not. **"You've lost weight" is how you tell a woman you like her.**

"Your hair looks great" used to be okay, but now may be interpreted as sexist. In fact, any and every comment concerning the body is potentially off-limits, given the current climate. Choose your comments carefully or you may be slapped—or worse, slapped with a lawsuit.

(Baldness is different. Some men never seem to accept it, or the toupee and weave industries wouldn't exist. But for the most part, men muddle through appropriate grieving stages. At the first signs of hair loss they lapse into denial. Then they feel sorry for themselves and make passes at temps. As more hair falls out, they slip further into denial, and then enter a period of coping, including comb-overs, Minoxidil, and secret forays to hair restorers. Finally, most return to sanity. The moment a man makes fun of his own hair loss marks the day you know he's dealt with it. He then has the opportunity to use it to his advantage, for any time you appear confident about something that might make another feel insecure, you come across as more powerful.)

The Evil Twin on physical appearance: It's the same as with clothes: The moment you see someone experimenting with a new hairstyle that makes her look like the Bride of Frankenstein, rave "Hey, great look."

Or try the Betty Crocker Maneuver: Selena is your arch-rival, Selena's on a diet, Selena's looking great, Selena's a chocoholic, and what do we have here? We just happen to have a freshly baked chocolate cake we wave in front of Selena's nose.

I once had an overweight friend who used to bring in mouth-watering cookies and cakes for the office every day. People thought she was an inveterate baker. She wasn't. She hated baking. It was her Evil Twin who slaved over the oven. The reason? No one would notice her weight problem if everyone else was equally hefty. The worst part was that it worked. Pound for pound, that office became the largest in Kansas City.

SPEAKING IN TONGUES

Louise and Henry had been married for several years before Henry ever visited his wife at her office. When he did, he found her—the only female—in midconversation with six male co-workers. That he didn't mind. He just couldn't believe what they were talking about.

"Give me a break," Louise was saying. "No way Pitino's going to turn the Celtics around in a year." Henry was hurt, since Louise had never professed any interest in sports at home. Later he asked her if she was having an affair. "How else would you even know Rick Pitino was a basketball coach?" he asked.

"If I didn't speak basketball," Louise said, "I couldn't hang around the guys who make the decisions."

People reveal themselves through their office language—not by their verbal ability or their education, but the degree to which they exhibit loyalty to the company's favorite jargon. You can't legally exclude anyone in the business world, but because exclusionary behavior is part of human nature, people will always find ways to engage in it. And language is a favorite means, since you can't get caught. So the in-crowd will have a more refined dialect, whether it's sports, sex, the armed forces, or any other subject that turns the Big Dogs on.

For instance: At Prudential Securities, a lot of the guys at the top were former Marines, and so they spoke Marine. "You can only eat what you kill," they'd say, and I had to have someone translate that for me ("Your pay is based on your direct contributions to the company"). "Good to go," they'd say, and I'd have it translated ("Ready").

It soon became evident that if I wanted to hang around with these guys, I had better learn how to speak pidgin Marine. It's not enough to understand what they're talking about. **You have to salute the language, and you have to act like you believe it.**

Acclimating to Wall Street involved using words I'd never dreamed of saying aloud regularly. The most obvious word was *fuck*, which was used as a noun, verb, adjective, and adverb. The classic sentence: An ex-soldier explaining to another that his radio was broken: "The fucking fucker is fucking fucked."

These days one of the more familiar forms of company in-speak is MBA talk. Therefore it's a good idea to keep up with the lingo peddled by business schools, which consider it their job to create new catchwords. These words come and go. *Synergy*, one of the big buzzwords of the '80s, is gone. *Downsizing* has turned into *right-sizing*. *Overhead value analysis* is passé, as is *reductions in force*.

Today words and phrases borrowed from technology are also fashionable. If you need something, you say, "That's a critical path for us." If you've got something that will make everyone buy a piece of hardware, you've got a "killer app" (as in applications): "The killer app of television was Milton Berle." If you want to redo a brochure, you don't edit it. You "repurpose the content," as in "Let's take this brochure and repurpose it for the Net."

Another common use of language is the Intimidating Vocabulary. I once worked with a man who would actually ask me if the quotidian directives of the chary apparatchiks were creating Weltschmerz. Few people knew what he was talking about, but we were all too scared to ask, since our confusion implied he was that much smarter than we were.

◆ The Evil Twin on language: If your worst enemy is trying to move in on your clique, the way to exclude him is to resort to your group's lingo, the way you might speak French in front of kids. For

instance, let's say Guy's uncomfortable talking about brand management (i.e., marketing the integrated image of the entire company
rather than its individual parts). Still, you need to discuss joint projects with him.

So you call a meeting stocked with your allies, then announce,
"We're here to talk today about brand management for the So-and-
So group, and we're going to start with line extensions and some kind
of global positioning, and whether or not we need to matrix responsibilities for this. Guy, would you start us off?"

We're now so deep into brand-marketing lingo, which Guy
doesn't speak, that Guy, in fact, can't speak.

YOU'RE NOT IN THE ARMY NOW

Somewhere in every large company is a group of people who behave as though the time were 1958 and the place were West Point. These guys salute stripes instead of people; they believe that anyone a few levels up in the ranks is always right. They assume their superiors possess, and always will possess, a sense of responsibility for them.

They're wrong. Business may have followed the army model forty years ago, because business organizations could once function on a command-and-control basis. But that's no longer the story.

Today's competitive, technology-rich, high-speed business environment requires flexibility. That's how companies succeed, and that kind of deftness typically means that no one's necessarily in complete command—or sometimes, even in control.

Yet a lot of the good old guys keep saluting, under the mistaken impression that it's always the right way to behave, which means that they're not thinking for themselves, which means that they're not flexible, and therefore, ultimately, they're fire-able. Then, when the ax falls, they moan, "But I was loyal; I saluted for thirty years." Too bad.

On a lesser level, this applies to anyone who thinks that obedience is invariably the answer. It isn't. If you think that your sole responsibility is to do your job, and that your job is the sum of a list of tasks you've been assigned, then you're at real risk of losing that job.

Some time ago I employed a young man named Carter, who defined his position as bookkeeper, although it could have encompassed more. Carter was satisfied only when someone else was telling him what to do. And he carried out orders to the letter. The problem was that not all situations come with orders. In Carter's case, a mistake related to bookkeeping arose, and it was one he could have spotted. But Carter focused only on his assigned work; no one told him to look for errors outside the immediate system, so he didn't.

Sure enough, things began to fall apart. It wasn't Carter's fault exactly, but it was clear to everyone that he should have seen it coming. Now everyone started calling him Poor Carter. He was transferred to a less-important division, and when that division was downsized, Poor Carter was one of the first let go. As far as he was concerned, he'd only done his job. But he wasn't paying attention to the larger world.

Important distinction: **Obedience is not the same thing as loyalty.** Obedience is fetching the stick, even if it's been thrown into a swamp. Loyalty is suggesting that a drained swamp would be easier to sell. When it's obedience, you blindly do whatever you're told, even if it's a stupid or dangerous idea. When it's loyalty, you challenge the command when you believe the command is flawed. This is a much higher level of support, because it carries risk. You know that your boss doesn't want to hear your complaints, but you're willing to complain nonetheless because you want to help him.

As with all rules, some flexibility is required. Sometimes you do have to shut up and be obedient. When your boss is in the middle of a battle, it's not a great time to bring up questions about K rations. I once had a subordinate who, whenever things got tough, would corner me to demand, "Is this a good time to talk about the company picnic? I wonder if we should try the shore this year." Fires were cropping up everywhere around us, and this man was droning on: "I'm not sure if we should do it right on the beach itself, but maybe we should think about this really great little resort I know. . . ."

There's yet another disadvantage to rank-and-file minds. They never know who's truly in power because they're always looking for the top name on the stationery instead of pinpointing who's actually calling the shots. Sometimes influence is so hidden that there is no stationery—or any other outward sign of power.

The best way to detect influence is to listen. The people with this kind of power are always being referred to in mysterious ways. "We should send Nathan a copy," they say. "Nathan would want to know that." If there's no other reason to let Nathan know what's going on except that everyone seems to feel it's necessary, no matter what rank Nathan holds, Nathan rules.

⟳ The Evil Twin on hierarchy: If you've decided that your company would be better off without your boss, feign abject obedience. The Big Guy is enamored of a project you know is worthless, and you're tired of trying to implement all of his bad ideas for him. So you say, "You've outdone yourself, Big Guy. This plan to spend half the budget on little yellow stickers is truly great."

There are two strong possibilities. One is that you're wrong about the little yellow stickers, and the Boss is actually right, and therefore you've helped put a good plan into motion. In that case, no problem.

On the other hand, if you're right, and he's wrong, he's going to be held accountable for his mistakes. You just want to make sure that you don't go down with him, which you can do by engaging in that time-honored political sport, Covering Your Butt (see same).

AFTERWORD

You may be tempted to write off office politics as complicated and unnecessary. But consider the alternative: no office politics.

The fantasy of an apolitical office conjures up some utopian paradise where everyone sees eye-to-eye and all work for the common good without having to deal with the tension of conflicting human desires.

That's simply not realistic. No utopia, whether communist, socialist, or transcendentalist, has ever worked. Office politics disappears only in the face of an overwhelming threat large enough to force people to put their agendas aside, or in a culture so repressive and authoritarian that obedience is the only means of survival.

In other words, office politics is a sign that the workplace is healthy, that the business is thriving, that the future is bright.

The truly terrible political battles don't take place at the office. They take place within your own mind, feeding on your insecurities, phobias, and suspicions.

Most people are defeated not by other people but by their reactions to other people. We become convinced that we're not going to get what we deserve, or we're afraid that someone else is going to take what is rightfully ours, whether it's a better office, a bigger salary, or even just that free taxi on a rainy day. In these tense situations, people begin to doubt themselves, which makes them feel overwhelmed and powerless. That, in turn, forces them to behave carelessly, acting in ways they later regret.

You only truly lose at politics when you declare it a loss. There will always be times when you didn't get that raise, when your rival landed the bigger office, when your assistant was promoted over your head. These things happen, but the trick is to move on. Each political loss can be recast as a gain; the score is never calculated until you've moved ahead and conquered something new. Then you can look back and think, "That wasn't a great move, but I learned enough from it to do better the next time."

The world is big, life is long, and as you master the art of office politics, you'll find that work, people and all, truly can be great.

ACKNOWLEDGMENTS

Unfortunately, most of the people smart enough to give me material for this book are too smart to want to be named. For all of you, a heartfelt thanks. You know who you are and we'll talk later.

Now, on to the people I can thank. My agent, Jan Miller, believed in this book when it was still a dream, and she made the dream come true. Everyone on her team offered support, and I'm grateful for their efforts.

I also want to thank Hyperion alumni Rick Kot, for acquiring the book; Brian DiFiore, for treating the book as if it were his own; and Mollie Doyle, who provided early hands-on assistance. Special thanks go to Jennifer Barth for her hard work and editorial talent.

In my career, I was fortunate enough to have tremendous guidance, especially from Bill and John; I also owe a great deal to Dr. Dee Soder, for her savvy career counsel and unending support. I was also blessed with extraordinary generosity from friends who shared professional expertise and contacts, including David, Rosie, Tank, Steve, and Flora's mom.

Finally, without my family, I wouldn't have had a career, and therefore no office politics. My late dad was one of my first bosses, and definitely my best. My brother, Myron, and my stepchildren, Amanda and Greg, all provided support during my midlife leap into a new career. And most of all, I have to thank my mom. All one-hundred pounds of her are will, and all of that will was behind me whenever I needed it. That has meant everything to me.